T0311247

Byzantium
Unbound

PAST IMPERFECT

Past Imperfect presents concise critical overviews of the latest research by the world's leading scholars. Subjects cross the full range of fields in the period ca. 400—1500 CE which, in a European context, is known as the Middle Ages. Anyone interested in this period will be enthralled and enlightened by these overviews, written in provocative but accessible language. These affordable paperbacks prove that the era still retains a powerful resonance and impact throughout the world today.

Director and Editor-in-Chief

Simon Forde, *'s-Hertogenbosch*

Production

Ruth Kennedy, *Adelaide*

Byzantium
Unbound

Anthony Kaldellis

ARC HUMANITIES PRESS

British Library Cataloguing in Publication Data
A catalogue record for this book is available from the British Library

© **2019, Arc Humanities Press, Leeds**

The author asserts their moral right to be identified as the author of this work.

Permission to use brief excerpts from this work in scholarly and educational works is hereby granted provided that the source is acknowledged. Any use of material in this work that is an exception or limitation covered by Article 5 of the European Union's Copyright Directive (2001/29/EC) or would be determined to be "fair use" under Section 107 of the U.S. Copyright Act September 2010 Page 2 or that satisfies the conditions specified in Section 108 of the U.S. Copyright Act (17 USC §108, as revised by P.L. 94-553) does not require the Publisher's permission.

ISBN (print): 9781641891998
e-ISBN (PDF): 9781641892001
e-ISBN (EPUB): 9781641892018

www.arc-humanities.org
Printed and bound by CPI Group (UK) Ltd, Croydon, CR0 4YY

Contents

Illustrations

Foreword

Byzantium has been pushed around a lot. Most overtly, as told in Chapter 1 below, it has been the target of western vilification and polemic starting from medieval times, going strong through the Enlightenment, and reaching all the way down to the twentieth century. Recent efforts to rehabilitate it have tended more to push back against bias than develop grounds for positive appreciation and engagement. But prim protests against bad words (such as "decline") will not spark interest among non-Byzantinists. More invidiously, as explained in Chapter 2, history has been carved up into periods in ways that often work to the disadvantage of Byzantium. For example, Byzantium has been artificially cut off from its Roman roots. Moreover, efforts by western medieval scholars to secure as western possessions the early Church Fathers (i.e., the Patristic period), the major Councils that defined the faith, and Justinian's codification of Roman law created another artificial scheme that left behind a rump Byzantium, starting in the seventh century. This appropriation has been revived recently in the invention of "late antiquity" as an (alleged) period and field of study.

This book exposes the history and politics of these biases but it also aims to lay a foundation for the positive study of Byzantium by historians and classicists. In doing so it proposes a long view of Byzantium, which begins in the early Roman empire, encompasses all the creative forces of the centuries after the foundation of Constantinople, and extends to the modern period. This is a Byzantium unbound by the interests of other cultures and fields of study that would cut it down to size to suit themselves. The aim of this book is not to advocate that such a "long view" be enshrined in textbooks, courses, and our general periodization. It is, instead, a thought-experiment in seeing the ancient Greek, Roman, and Christian traditions as flowing together, without great ruptures, to form this one particular civilization, and only this one. It presents Byzantium as an unparalleled vantage-point from which we can look back to ancient history and forward to modernity, as well as west to the origins of Europe and east to the Islamic world, without great obstructions in one's field of vision. It is only a start: much more can, should, and hopefully will be said. To be sure, it is also impossible to present new ways of looking at history without being provocative: that is part of the book by design.

The book is not a potted history of Byzantium (there are plenty of those in print these days). The basics can be stated here briefly. Readers who are already familiar with the basic history can skip the next two pages. Also, except where otherwise specified, I use the term "medieval" to refer to western Europe between 500 and 1500, roughly to wherever Latin was the learned language and the churches owed allegiance to Rome; I mean it in distinction to Byzantium and its own cultural orbit, as Chapter 4 will argue.

What we call Byzantium was nothing other than the direct continuation of the Roman empire in the east. A Roman empire had existed in the Greek east since the second century BC and included the entire eastern Mediterranean by the end of the first century BC. (I will employ the BC/AD convention for calendar eras, numerically equivalent to the BCE/CE convention.) The eastern empire acquired its own capital, Constantinople or New Rome, in 330 AD, half a millennium after the Roman conquest of Greece and Asia Minor and a century after the universal extension of Roman citizenship in 212 AD. The fall of the western empire during the course of the fifth century left the east as the only remaining Roman empire. Its population of around twenty million included, in addition to a majority of Greek-speakers, a large number of Coptic-speakers in Egypt, Aramaic-speakers in Palestine and Syria, and Latin-speakers in the Balkans. The empire was about half Christian and half pagan in 400 AD, but the balance shifted in the Christian direction rapidly after that. In the sixth century, the eastern empire made a remarkable resurgence under the emperor Justinian (527–565), a Latin-speaker from the Balkans, whose armies reconquered North Africa, Italy, and parts of Spain. Justinian also built Hagia Sophia and codified Roman law, but his reign witnessed the outbreak of a deadly plague, his wars devastated important provinces, and his intolerance led to outbreaks of severe religious persecution.

In the seventh century, after a long and destructive war with Persia, which it won, the empire lost Palestine, Syria, Egypt, and eventually North Africa to the emergent Muslim armies. At the same time, the Balkan provinces were taken over by the Avars, a nomadic warrior empire, followed by the Bulgars and the Slavs, who settled in many regions south of the Danube. After these developments, the Roman empire became more homogeneously Greek-speaking and unified in its religious confession (Christian, accepting the Council of Chalcedon of 451 AD), but no less Roman than before. It began a gradual process of administrative reform and territorial consolidation. By the ninth century, it had reabsorbed much of Greece back into its provincial governance along with southern Italy. Arab attacks were successfully fended off, though raids continued until the later tenth century, when the empire went on the offensive. Under a series of military emperors, it conquered Cilicia, Antioch, and parts of northern Syria, a number of Armenian and Georgian principalities in the Caucasus, and, in 1018, the Bulgarian empire too, after a long and bitter war. This was the peak of Roman power in what we call the middle Byzantine period.

This power collapsed when the Normans conquered southern Italy (between the 1040s and 1071) and the Seljuk Turks conquered Asia Minor (in the 1070s), which had for many centuries been the heartland of the Roman world. The empire proved to be resilient, as before, and managed to gain back western (coastal) Asia Minor in the late 1090s with the help of an invited western army, known as the First Crusade. The twelfth century witnessed a remarkable revival of literature written in the archaic idiom of classical Greek favoured by Byzantine writers. This included histories, orations, romance novels, and classical scholarship. At the same time, a rift had been growing between the Churches of Rome and Constantinople, also known as the Latin and Greek Churches, today the Catholic and Orthodox Churches. The easterners rejected the papal claim of supremacy within the global Church, while westerners grew increasingly suspicious of the east Romans, whom they snidely called "Greeks." Also, the emerging neo-Roman political ideology of western Europe made no allowances for the eastern empire and eastern Romans (a bias that continues to this day in the West). This hostility culminated in the capture and destruction of Constantinople by the Fourth Crusade in 1204, whose soldiers destroyed a large part of its artistic and literary patrimony. This calculated atrocity doomed future efforts to establish union between these two halves of the Christian world.

The Crusaders had planned to divide up the entire empire and distribute it among their own lordships and states. However, the Romans regrouped in three separate states of their own, in Epeiros (western Greece), Nikaia (northwestern Asia Minor), and Trebizond. The state at Nikaia eventually managed to recapture the capital, Constantinople, in 1261, and reconstitute the empire, albeit it was a pale reflection of its former self. It lost Asia Minor by the end of the thirteenth century, but regained ground in Greece and the Balkans. Still, it was squeezed between Turkish emirates and Latin principalities, as well as by Serbs, Bulgarians, and Albanians. The empire held on until 1453, when its capital was taken by the armies of the Ottoman sultan Mehmet II. Outposts survived in the Peloponnese and the independent state of Trebizond, but these succumbed as well in the 1460s. Thus did the monarchy established by Caesar and Augustus come to an end. Yet the Roman people, their language, and their Church survived under Ottoman rule all the way to the twentieth century.

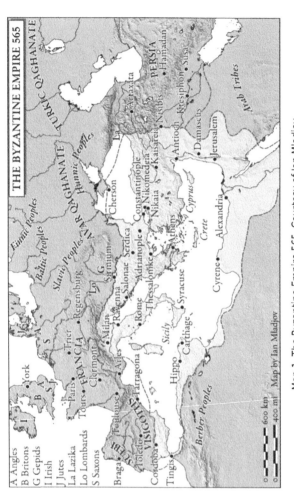

Map 1. The Byzantine Empire 565. Courtesy of Ian Mladjov.

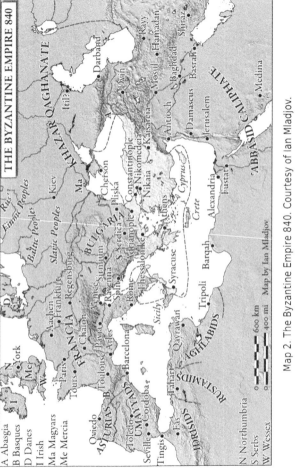

Map 2. The Byzantine Empire 840. Courtesy of Ian Mladjov.

Chapter 1

A History of Byzantinophobia

What things are called is incomparably more important than what they are. The reputation, name, and appearance, the usual measure and weight of a thing, what it counts for—originally almost always wrong and arbitrary, thrown over things like a dress and altogether foreign to their nature and even to their skin—all this grows from generation unto generation, merely because people believe in it, until it gradually grows to be part of the thing and turns into its very body. What at first was appearance becomes in the end, almost invariably, the essence and is effective as such.

Nietzsche, *The Gay Science* 2.58 (trans. W. Kaufmann)

For a civilization that did relatively little harm, prized humility and compassion, preserved its existence and integrity against overwhelming odds, and contributed in captivating ways to the diversity of human culture, Byzantium is oddly one of the most maligned and misunderstood civilizations of the past. Its greatness and true nature were buried under so many layers of western prejudice, polemic, and deceit that for centuries only an invidious caricature was visible from outside. Westerners who actually visited it were just as likely to come away amazed by it as to have their prior prejudices confirmed, and even after its fall one could see through some of the distortions, at least with the benefits of scholarly training. But over time more coats of prejudice were added on rather than stripped away. As late as the mid-twentieth century, Byzantium was encased like an onion in multiple layers of hardened distortion, each dating from a different period of western imagination, fantasy, and politics. Only in the previous generation has a systematic effort been mounted to peel these stereotypes away, though the effort has been partial, is often uninspiring, and has sometimes added to the problem.

It is unnecessary and even hard to get personally worked up about this injustice. Arguably no one is directly harmed by it today, and there are too many pressing problems in the world that deserve our outrage, including lethal racism, neo-feudal economic inequality, the erosion of free society, and the fact that we are wrecking our only habitat in the universe. Nevertheless, you, the reader, would not be starting this book unless you were interested in Byzantium and what it means to us. So let us indulge this esoteric interest. The size and format of this book makes it easy for you to take it along to the protest or rally of your choice.

I will start at the beginning and trace the growth of this monster onion from the inside out, as each new layer enveloped the previous one. Indeed, the innermost layers have become almost invisible. Our focus here is on the image of Byzantium in the West, which eventually gave birth to the academic field of Byzantine Studies. Byzantium has a slightly different image in Greece, where it has been fitted (rather awkwardly) into the national story, and in the Slavic Orthodox countries, which derive their religion and a great deal of their culture from it. It has a significantly different image in Muslim countries, in many respects a more honourable one.

Roman Denialism

The original sin around which subsequent layers of distortion began to accrue was what I have called "Roman denialism." This was the (successful) attempt by leaders, institutions, and writers in medieval Europe to deny that the eastern empire was what it always claimed to be—i.e., the empire of the Romans—and to deny that its majority population were who they claimed to be, i.e., Romans in an ethnic and not just a formal legal sense. A word of background is here necessary.

After the fall of the western Roman empire in the fifth century, its provinces were occupied by Germanic warrior-bands with their own kings: Goths in Spain, Lombards in much of Italy, Franks in Gaul, and Anglo-Saxons in Britain. The city of Rome, by contrast, was under eastern control between the sixth and the eighth centuries, and its bishop (the pope) was a minor figure in its imperial periphery. In his letter to emperor Konstantinos IV and the Church Council of Constantinople in 680, pope Agatho humbly offered obedience on behalf of himself, "this Roman city that is subject to your most Serene Power,"[1] and all the western nations that might one day come under the rule of the most Christian emperor.

Until the eighth century, everyone in the West recognized the empire of Constantinople as *the* Roman empire. Rulers as far as Spain recognized that the eastern court was the heir of Romulus, and a writer in Ireland (Adomnan of Iona) called Constantinople "the capital of the Roman empire." While they did not see themselves as its direct subjects, the post-Roman kingdoms of the West regarded the eastern empire as an ancient and more prestigious state from which they too might seek validation along with symbols and practices of kingship. They turned to Constantinople in order to understand ancient Roman customs.

This changed during the eighth century. The city of Rome slipped out of imperial control, and its Church (the papacy) developed a more exalted sense of its role in history, now as the Roman Republic of St. Peter. The popes sought secular patrons among the Franks, who had created a large empire in northwestern and central Europe. This rapprochement culminated in the coronation by the pope of Charlemagne as Roman emperor, in Rome in 800 AD. The Roman imperial title would be used fitfully by western rulers during the next two centuries—they did not really know what it meant in a Frankish context—but they used it more consistently and emphat-

---

I Pope Agatho, *Letter 1 to the August Emperors*, ed. J.-P. Migne, Patrologiae Cursus Completus Series Latina, 212 vols. (Paris: Migne, 1841–65), 87:col. 1163B.

ically after the eleventh century. Eventually, it gave rise to the Holy Roman Empire of the German Nation, which abolished itself in 1806 under pressure by Napoleon, who also invoked ancient Roman precedents when he crowned himself "Empereur." Meanwhile, the medieval papacy had developed its own theories of Romanness and empire, according to which the pope was the arbiter of both. This resulted in famous clashes between the medieval popes and the German emperors over the ownership and adjudication of imperial titles and the Roman legacy.

Those clashes between popes and German emperors fill up the view of all medievalists interested in the problem of empire in the Middle Ages. But they are beside the point here. What matters for us is that both the popes and the Germans agreed that the eastern empire—our "Byzantium"—had effectively lost its rights to the Roman name. They developed various silly theories as to why Constantinople ceased being Roman—for example, that its ruler at the time of Charlemagne's coronation was a woman (Eirene), and women don't count, therefore the throne was effectively vacant and could be reassigned to the Franks by the pope; or that the eastern empire could not be Roman because it did not hold the city of Rome (of course, neither did any German emperor). These and other pretexts were made up to serve an ideological point, as was the notion that there could be only one emperor at a time (in ancient Rome and Byzantium there could be co-emperors who shared power). But western Europe went on to develop complex theories of empire, politics, and law from which Constantinople was largely excluded, for it had (allegedly) irrevocably lost its Romanness.

These theories of empire, which eventually became the western tradition of political thought, were never fully satisfactory. The pope, for example, usually held Rome but did not have an empire, whereas the German king might have entitled himself "emperor of the Romans" but could never explain who these Romans were of whom he was supposed to be the emperor; he rarely held the city of Rome, for instance, and never governed it. The emperor in Constantinople, by contrast, ruled in direct succession from the ancient emperors; lived in a city formally called New Rome since its foundation by Constantine the Great; and the vast majority of his subjects considered themselves as ethnic Romans (or *Romaioi*, in Greek). Yet this state was routinely excluded from western debates about Romanness and empire (and is often still excluded). Thus, in their correspondence with Constantinople, the popes and the German emperors frequently refused to use the correct title for the eastern emperor and called him instead the emperor of the Greeks, the emperor of Constantinople, or (at best) the emperor of New Rome. On one occasion, the eastern court was so infuriated when a papal letter arrived calling Nikephoros II Phokas (963–969) "the emperor of the Greeks" that he threw the papal emissaries into prison.[2]

A few western cities, kings, and writers can be found after 900 AD who explicitly recognized the easterners for what they were, Romans, but these were a small minority. There were also a number of royal courts in the west that copied contemporary Byzantine practices in their efforts to look imperial or more Roman, rather than hunt for them among the ruins of antiquity. But that acknowledgment of Byzantium's imperial prestige was mostly implicit: it resulted in no theory that could sustain the eastern empire's claims. In the mainstream western tradition, out of which the discipline of Byzantine Studies later emerged, it is a foundational belief that "Byzantium" did not have a Roman "essence," that it had somehow mutated into something else, despite what its own people said. This weird belief persists today and can quickly be spotted by anyone who reads scholarship on Byzantium. For example, there is the evasive phrase that "the Byzantines called themselves Romans," an acknowledgment of the truth that enables the modern historian to wriggle out of calling them Romans herself. Often, the fact that the Byzantines called themselves Romans is labelled "paradoxical"

---

2 Liudprand, *Embassy to Constantinople* 47 (full reference in the Further Reading for Chapter 1).

or "technical" or "delusional." Flimsy arguments are still set forth for why the Byzantines were not "really" Romans as they believed, such as that they were Christians, or because they had eunuchs, or because their empire was too small, and so on. These are but modern parallels of the medieval idea that Byzantium lost its Roman rights when it placed a woman on the throne.[3]

I am aware of no other culture that, in the twenty-first century, is studied in such a bizarre way. For which other people do we acknowledge that they called themselves by a specific group name, but then we add that they weren't really what they thought they were but were only "deceiving themselves" or "trying to deceive us" by saying it? Even those claims are sometimes made, nonsensical though they are. Fortunately, there are honourable exceptions to this tradition of denialism, including John Bagnell Bury, Steven Runciman, and Hans-Georg Beck, who wrote about Byzantium as a Roman civilization, but their approach has not been followed widely.

Roman denialism is the original sin of Byzantinism in the West. It has led to a distorted view of who the Byzantines were and to a desperate search for made-up alternatives to fill the void left by denial of the truth. It has also hindered original research that would unlock fascinating *Roman* aspects of their culture and history. In fact, it has stunted and stultified the field, locking it into a permanent state of cognitive dissonance. Denialism literally makes professional Byzantinists unable to give a straight answer to the question of who the Byzantines really were, when, in contrast, our sources are quite clear about it. At the same time, it has created a curious double-standard within Medieval Studies. A moderate level of interest on the part of a medieval count in some aspect of the Roman political tradition can earn him the reputation in modern scholarship for being a "Neo-Roman."[4] But the Byz-

---

3 Citations in A. Kaldellis, *Romanland: Ethnicity and Empire in Byzantium* (Cambridge, MA: Harvard University Press, 2019).

4 B. S. Bachrach, "Neo-Roman vs. Feudal: The Heuristic Value of

antines, for whose Romanness we have mounds of evidence and who literally called themselves Romans in direct continuation of the Romans of antiquity, are excluded from this discussion. The underlying truth is that they are not part of the story that western Europe wants to tell about itself.

Stereotypes of Greek Ethnicity

But if the Byzantines were not "really" Romans, who were they? The alternative answer given by medieval popes and German emperors was that they were ethnic Greeks. This is the second layer in our onion. Now, there was no problem in calling the eastern Romans "Greek-speakers," because they were: they sometimes called themselves *Graikoi* in such a linguistic sense (though not often). But it was quite a different matter to conclude from this that they were ethnic Greeks, which is precisely what western medieval writers began to assume. Witness a letter sent by Louis II, great-grandson of Charlemagne and German emperor in Italy, to the Byzantine emperor Basileios I in 871.[5] In order to argue that Basileios I, his subjects, and empire were not genuinely Roman, which is the point of the letter, Louis cites as evidence the fact that the eastern empire existed among people who spoke Greek, not Latin; that their ethnic and cultural makeup was Greek, not Roman; and that they did not hold the city of Rome. This was not an argument that Louis was making after a careful consideration of the evidence from antiquity about who could or could not be Roman. (In antiquity, there was no requirement that one speak Latin in order to be a Roman, and plenty of Greek-speakers were Romans and vice versa.) It was instead an ad hoc argument designed to exclude the Byzantines from

a Construct for the Reign of Fulk Nerra, Count of the Angevins (987–1040)," *Cithara* 30 (1990): 3–30.

5 In *Epistolae Karolini aevi, V*, ed. E. Caspar, G. Laehr et al., Monumenta Germaniae Historica. Epistolae 7 (Berlin: Weidmann, 1928): 385–94.

a share in the Roman tradition, which Louis wanted to claim exclusively for himself.

In order to properly understand a culture, the politicized opinions of its rivals should matter less for us. We need instead to focus on how it viewed its own identity, including the names, signs, stories, and cultural practices that it valued. If we follow this approach, we find that the Byzantines rejected the idea that they were Greeks, first because they directly said so themselves in response to western claims, and also because they viewed the Greeks (or Hellenes) as a pagan nation of the ancient world. As far as they knew, there were no ethnic Hellenes left in the world. Now, in the vocabulary of the eastern Church, the term Hellene was also used generically for "pagans," but the Byzantines were not that either. They were Christian Romans and, in their histories, they traced the origin of their polity and society back to Rome and Troy, which was the standard Roman narrative. They correctly saw their state as the only surviving direct continuation of the ancient Roman *res publica* and empire. Their laws, government, armies, national polity, and name were Roman and derived from Rome. They called their state *Romanía*, i.e., "Romanland." This term was used unofficially at first (starting around 300 AD), but by the tenth–eleventh centuries it was being used by the court as the official name for the state.

Louis' argument about the Greekness of Byzantium, which seemed only commonsensical to medieval writers, was based on the idea that identity was defined by ancestry and language. Therefore, Greek-speakers in lands where the ancient Greeks used to live were also "Greeks." This was superficially plausible and rhetorically effective. It was good enough for western purposes. But it was not at all how Romans saw things, whether in antiquity or Byzantium. Ancient Rome had famously absorbed people from a wide variety of ethnic backgrounds into its polity and made them into Romans. Ancestry had never defined or limited Roman identity. Nor was speaking Latin a requirement for being Roman in antiquity. Greek had been a language of Roman culture from the start. The ancient Roman elite spoke Greek, Rome was a city whose second language was Greek—remember that St. Paul wrote his letter to the Christian community at Rome in Greek—and the Romans had governed their eastern provinces in Greek for many centuries before those provinces were the only empire they had left. Even Roman law had shifted from Latin to Greek during the sixth century, after which Italians had to search for rough Latin translations of new laws, an ironic reversal. Therefore, there was nothing un-Roman about a Greek-speaking Rome. But popes, German kings, and their spokesmen in the Middle Ages defined the Roman tradition as essentially Latinate, and to promote that idea they excluded the Byzantines from it as *Graeci*.

Having defined the Byzantines as Greeks, the Latins then proceeded to pile on negative ethnic stereotypes about them. Ancient Latin literature gave off mixed signals about the Greeks. The ancient Romans had admired Hellenic philosophy, art, language, and glorious history, but found contemporary Greeks—the ones with whom they were frequently at war—to be soft, pedantic, rather decadent, politically subservient, and sexually troubling. In formulating negative views of the Greeks, the Romans had ironically recycled some of the stereotypes that the Greeks had themselves once applied to eastern barbarians, such as the Persians. These were now recycled in the medieval West to tar the "Greeks" of the eastern empire as treacherous, faithless, fickle, and unreliable; as soft and delicate scribblers of words rather than stout warriors (Byzantine society was more literate than any place in western Europe, and less violent); and sexually as less than full men, diminished by the powerful role of eunuchs at the court and eastern Church.

To be sure, these views were not universal. There were also westerners who admired the Byzantines and the virtues of their civilization, which was in many ways more advanced than any culture in the West. But these exceptional observers wrote few texts and played a small role in shaping western images of Byzantium. By the time of the Fourth Crusade (1204 AD), there was a fully developed image in place of the Byzantines as weak, degenerate, and faithless mannequins.

The conquest and destruction of Constantinople by the soldiers of the Fourth Crusade confirmed that image and locked it in place. The hardy (Catholic) Romans of the West had once again triumphed over the quibbling (Orthodox) Greeks of the east, bringing them (or so they hoped) under the direction of the Church of Rome. This was even seen by some in the West as Roman payback for the Greek conquest of Troy!

Western writers routinely compared the Byzantines to women: *quasi femina Graecus* was a typical insult. It was also falsely reported that the Greek emperor castrated the sons of his nobles and prostituted their daughters in order to seduce French knights and not to have to fight them. These were orientalist fantasies of sexualized difference. Odo of Deuil, a participant and historian of the Second Crusade, wrote that

> Constantinople is arrogant in her wealth, treacherous in her practices, corrupt in her faith; just as she fears everyone on account of her wealth, she is dreaded by everyone on account of her treachery and faithlessness. If she did not have these vices, however, she would be preferable to all other places.[6]

That last clause, amusing though it is in context, reveals the great admiration that Constantinople could excite in western visitors. No city in the West could adequately prepare them for its wealth, size, population, sophisticated governance, and monuments. But their armies still destroyed it in 1204.

To be fair, the Byzantines developed negative stereotypes of the Latins as well, especially after the astonishing brutality of the Fourth Crusade. One scholar has cleverly observed that whereas the Latins attributed to the Byzantines the vices of arrogant women, the Byzantines inversely attributed to the Latins the vices of uncivilized men: anger, unthinking violence, a lack of learning, and insatiable greed.[7]

---

6 Odo of Deuil, *De profectione Ludovici VII in Orientem: The Journey of Louis VII to the East*, ed. and trans. V. G. Berry (New York: Norton, 1948), 87.

7 C. Messis, "Lectures sexuées de l'altérité: les Latins et identité

The relationship was almost like a dysfunctional and violent domestic quarrel. But, as always, masculine brutality did far more damage here than its feminine counterpart.

Religious Polemic and the Fourth Crusade

Ethnic stereotypes were made worse by religious polemic. The Churches of Rome and Constantinople had never fully seen eye-to-eye, ever since the fourth century in fact, and their practices diverged over time, as was to be expected from institutions that operated in different languages, under dissimilar political circumstances, and among populations with diverse ethnic and cultural backgrounds. By the ninth century, deviations in doctrine, stemming from words added to the Latin Creed, and the popes' claim on supreme jurisdiction within the Church, exacerbated what were otherwise innocuous differences in practice. This led to flare-ups of hostility and even to mutual accusations of heresy. The patriarch Photios of Constantinople (858–867, 877–886) liked to point out where the Church of Rome had gone wrong, a habit that angered a number of popes. Another round of mutual recriminations followed in 1054, when papal legates sent to Constantinople to conclude a military alliance excommunicated the patriarch Michael Keroularios (1043–1059) and he had to respond in kind. By this time the papacy had entered its Reformist phase: Rome was insisting that it had the sole and absolute power to decide all religious questions for the whole of Christendom, and claimed jurisdiction over all churches. Keroularios did not see things that way, of course, nor did any other Byzantine.

In reality, even before the eleventh century the Churches of Rome and Constantinople held contradictory, conflicting, or just different beliefs about many aspects of belief and practice, including clerical celibacy, the use of leavened or unleavened bread in communion, and the doctrine of the procession of the Holy Spirit from within the Trinity. To make

romaine menacée pendant les derniers siècles de Byzance," *Jahrbuch der österreichischen Byzantinistik* 61 (2011): 151–70.

matters worse, they also lacked an agreed-upon mechanism for resolving differences, as they disagreed about jurisdictional issues too. One could say, then, that the two Churches were already in a state of Schism, which explained the aforementioned spate of recriminations and excommunications. But even so they did not want to believe that they were in a state of schism. As each outbreak of hostilities died down, they normalized relations and carried on diplomatically as if they were not divided by a widening gap. But the damage was slowly being done: many of the warriors of the Fourth Crusade were convinced that the "Greeks" were heretics.

The tacit agreement-to-disagree in matters of the faith did not survive the carnage of the Fourth Crusade. Theologians and polemicists in both Churches had been getting louder in condemning the other side as "schismatic" or downright "heretical." In the West, there was a long-standing tradition of blaming the Greek East for the origin of all major heresies that had troubled the Church since ancient times. Whereas Greek-speakers found Latin to be a "narrow" language, incapable of expressing fine conceptual distinctions, some Latin Christians believed that Greeks were too smart for their own good: the subtleties of their language led them to keep inventing new heresies. Many increasingly called for the East to be "restored" to the good order and discipline of the Church of Rome, and it was particularly unlucky that this movement coincided with the Crusades. Now, the eastern empire had assisted the First Crusade and even made it possible in the first place: this was the only one of the Crusades that succeeded in its stated goals. Yet after it relations between the empire and the Crusaders deteriorated with each new wave. The passage of armies in a context of mutual suspicion is not a good recipe for cultural understanding. The Byzantines suspected that the Crusaders had evil intentions against their empire—time would prove them horribly correct about this—whereas some Latins suspected that the "perfidious Greeks" were plotting with the Muslims against the Crusaders (as indeed, sometimes they were). Certainly, the Byzantines were unenthusiastic about the later Crusades.

The rift widened, the "Greeks" were denounced as heretics, and eventually a Crusade was "diverted" to Constantinople.

The city's destruction in 1204 was seen by the pope as an unfortunate accident but also as an opportunity to restore the Greek Church to "obedience." By this point, attitudes on both sides had hardened. The Byzantines began to circulate lists of the errors and heresies of the Latins, while Catholic writers produced treatises *Contra errores Graecorum* (*Against the Errors of the Greeks*). The western Church was now perceived by most Byzantines as the single greatest threat to their faith and identity. The papacy tried to impose Catholicism on the occupied territories, which only exacerbated tensions and defined the differences between the Churches more sharply. The ideal of Union never died; indeed, it still lives on today. But despite many attempts to define it, and after countless councils and proclamations that it has finally been achieved, true Union remains ineluctably beyond reach. The Fourth Crusade left behind it, in all Orthodox countries, a deep suspicion of any "idealistic" campaign of western armies whether on behalf of all Christians or, as in modern times, to "safeguard human rights." The problems caused by the Crusades abide, not merely between Christian and Muslims lands but between Orthodox and Catholic ones as well.

Religious polemic, therefore, added another dimension of hostility to the western prejudice against the Greeks. Indeed, it was easy to believe that the Greeks deserved the horror of 1204 because their deviant religious beliefs had angered God. In fourteenth-century Italy, the proto-humanist Petrarch condemned the Greeks for deviating from the teachings and discipline of the Roman Church and also for daring to call themselves "Romans." For him, true Romans were Italians who spoke Latin and had conquered the world through their valour; those "little Greeks," by contrast were the Romans' justly enslaved subjects.[8]

---

8 N. Bisaha, *Creating East and West: Renaissance Humanists and the Ottoman Turks* (Philadelphia: University of Pennsylvania Press, 2004), 118–22.

Stigmatized by Failure

Byzantium was irrevocably stigmatized by failure when its capital city was conquered by the Ottoman Turks in 1453 and its empire was extinguished. By then, many Latins were actually fighting to save Byzantium from the infidel, who was advancing into Catholic lands too and was poised to invade Europe (or so they feared). Many westerners, forgetting what their own armies had done in 1204, lamented the cruelties inflicted by the Turks on the Greeks. But many also blamed the Greeks for not adhering to the terms of Church Union dictated by the West, and their empire was long regarded as a historical dead end anyway. It had not been Roman to begin with, and, by the time of the Ottoman conquest, it was but a tiny kingdom reduced to a dilapidated city and some islands, surrounded by Serbs, Albanians, Bulgarians, and Turks. Many humanists, for all that they admired ancient Greece, believed that the Greeks of their own time fully deserved their sad fate.

Early modern Europeans had other things to worry about in their rapidly changing world than the dim memory of the now extinct "empire of the Greeks." There were the controversies of the Renaissance, the discovery of the New World, the Reformation, Counter-Reformation, scientific revolution, wars of religion, and so on. Controversy, however, has a way of generating new and even unintended perspectives. For example, Martin Luther attacked the Catholic doctrine according to which the pope had taken the Roman imperial title away from the Greeks and transferred it to the Germans, arguing that the pope could never have transferred what never belonged to him in the first place.[9] A Byzantine would absolutely have agreed, but Luther was not defending Byzantium. He still pigeon-holed it as "Greek." His goal was to take down papal claims.

---

9 Martin Luther, *Three Treatises*, trans. C. M. Jacobs, A. T. W. Steinhaeuser, and W. A. Lambert (Philadelphia: Muhlenberg, 1947), 101–3.

When they looked east in the fifteenth and sixteenth centuries, Europeans had to contend with the advance of Ottoman armies, which reached all the way to Vienna on a few occasions. The former Greek empire also became a topic fit for antiquarian research, which was pursued in various niches of the scholarly world. In publications, which included editions and collections of historical texts, it was still called the empire of the Greeks or the empire of Constantinople, but sometimes the adjectival form "Byzantine" was used as well. "Byzantion" was an archaic name used by the "Greeks" themselves to refer to their capital (only), so in western usage the term "Byzantine empire" was tantamount to saying "empire of Constantinople." But the dominant label at this time remained the Greek one, carrying its negative ethnic and religious baggage and now tainted additionally by the stigma of failure and enslavement.

Byzantine history was a niche interest among early modern scholars, but there were moments when it came to the fore. Scholars at the court of Louis XIV used the Greek empire as a possible model (among many others) for the grand aspirations and world-historical role assumed by the French crown. Byzantine texts were translated and published, including manuals of advice for kings, and prestige Byzantine objects signifying piety and power were circulated and collected. But the fundamentals of the western perception ("perfidious decadent Greeks") were not challenged. They were rather reinforced during this era by the reports of European travellers who began to visit Greek-speaking Orthodox lands in the east. Many of these travellers were mostly interested in classical Greece and were shocked by the contrast between what they had imagined, based on their education, and what they saw before them in Greece, or they pretended to be shocked for literary effect: ruined temples plundered to build small churches; poverty and squalor everywhere; no memory of Attic Greek but instead the "corrupt" vernacular of spoken Greek, which the locals called "Romaic" (i.e., "the Roman tongue"); communities led by illiterate local priests; superstition, fear, and ignorance of antiquity; and none of the political virtues and aspirations toward greatness for which European elites prided themselves. It was natural for them to associate the squalor that they saw with the Orthodox tradition generally, including Byzantium, and to theorize it as the great corruptor and destroyer of the ancient world. Byzantium had caused the Greeks to fall from the heights of Perikles to the baseness of superstitious slaves of the Ottoman Turks. The "Greek empire" was now imagined as just a medieval version of the contemporary Ottoman empire.

We can see this transference in the great history of Byzantium written in the later eighteenth century by Edward Gibbon, *The Decline and Fall of the Roman Empire*. Writing about the "Greek empire" of the fourteenth century, he digresses out of curiosity to discuss the state of contemporary Athens, and cribs his account from contemporary travel writers:

> By some, who delight in the contrast, the modern language of Athens is represented as the most corrupt and barbarous of the seventy dialects of the vulgar Greek [...] it would not be easy, in the country of Plato and Demosthenes, to find a reader or a copy of their works. The Athenians walk with supine indifference among the glorious ruins of antiquity; and such is the debasement of their character, that they are incapable of admiring the genius of their predecessors (chap. 62).

An impression was thus formed of Greek Orthodox civilization as corrupt, degenerate, and indifferent to the virtues of classical antiquity, a view that could not but be projected back onto Byzantium itself as well. All this was, however, a politically expedient view on the part of western travellers and may well have been distorted for a particular reason. Many of those travellers were seeking to acquire classical artworks and manuscripts of ancient authors, some of which they came by in underhanded ways. It served their interests to pretend, or even to believe, that the locals from whom they were buying, swindling, or just stealing these precious monuments of antiquity were ignorant of their value, indeed that they feared them because "ancient demons" lurked in their vicinity, and that they begged the fearless Europeans to take them away! It was thus advantageous to claim that the country was populated by ignorant monks and illiterate priests. We now know that this was not necessarily true, and that many local communities prized their ancient ruins and books greatly. But the basic idea that Greek Orthodox people were not interested in classical art and literature and even feared it for superstitious reasons was embedded in western perceptions, and was still being projected by scholars onto Byzantium well into the late twentieth century. Even today scholars can be found who believe that the Byzantine attitude toward classical antiquity was a mixture of ignorance, indifference, or superstitious fear. But surely this cannot explain why they preserved classical literature or why their capital was a museum of classical art (see Chapter 3).

Early modern travellers were not, of course, encountering Byzantium in Ottoman Greece, though some of them may have confused the two. What they were seeing were the long-term effects of the degradation of enslavement and loss of political autonomy caused by centuries of Ottoman rule. This filter interposed by the Ottomans still remains invisible, yet it fundamentally shaped perceptions of Byzantium in the West. The sultans dismantled the political institutions of the empire that they conquered and left in place only its Church and monasteries, into whose hands they entrusted the local governance of Orthodox communities. In this environment, religious texts, archives, and even buildings had greater chances of survival than secular ones, and community leadership passed into the hands of mostly clerical authorities. Secular education was nearly extinguished. Observers were therefore left with a skewed image of life under the Orthodox empire. They never actually met a Byzantine general, statesman, or administrator, or indeed any of the learned Byzantine bishops from the provinces (such as Arethas or Michael Choniates) whose classical learning and knowledge of ancient Greek dwarfed that of any early modern European scholar. Instead, they met allegedly ignorant monks and illiterate local priests, further tainting their view of Byzantium.

Polemics of the Enlightenment

The reputation of Byzantium was brought to its nadir by the thinkers of the European Enlightenment in the eighteenth century. Some of them, such as Voltaire and Rousseau, simply poured out torrents of abuse against the Greek empire. They regarded its history as nothing but a succession of worthless miracles, debauchery, villainy, and murder. For Hegel the eastern empire was "highly civilized" yet still nothing more than

> a millennial series of uninterrupted crimes, weaknesses, basenesses and want of principle; a most repulsive and consequently a most uninteresting picture [...] persisting in blind obedience to the patriarchs and the priesthood... wretched, insane passions stifling the growth of all that was noble; rebellion on the part of generals, and assassinations or poisoning of the emperors by their own wives and sons.[10]

The analyses of Roman decline by the political theorist Montesquieu (d. 1755) and the still-magnificent historian Edward Gibbon (d. 1792) were more nuanced and less reliant on outright insult when they reached the Byzantine period, but they still affirmed at their core the negative view of the Greek empire that pervaded their intellectual milieu. They saw it as a manifestation of Roman decline and sought to understand the reasons for its failure. To be sure, even this approach had the merit of treating it as a worthy topic of study and, indeed, as an extension of the history of Rome, but from a distance of over two centuries we can now see the cultural politics at work in Enlightenment theorizing—even in Gibbon, though he is a more complex case as he delved deeply into the minutiae of Byzantine history.

The thinkers of the Enlightenment were social reformers. In the name of reason and progress, they wanted to condemn and abolish many aspects of their own civilization which they

---

10 G. W. F. Hegel, *The Philosophy of History*, trans. J. Sibree (Mineola: Dover, 1956), 338.

believed were relics of a bygone irrational age, especially clerical authority, the alliance of throne and altar, and the stultifying effects of religious education such as dogmatism and fanaticism. It was, however, extremely dangerous and even illegal to attack the powerful men and institutions that embodied those forces in their own societies. It was therefore safer for them to set up historical surrogates for those problems and attack them instead. The imaginary "Byzantium" that many Enlightenment thinkers criticized was precisely such a proxy target. It stood for the violent despotism and complete lack of civic virtue to which theocracy and superstitious fanaticism was bound to lead any society. Byzantium was the despised Other that stood for a covert inner enemy. Conversely, Montesquieu and Voltaire both wrote positively—absurdly positively—about England as a way of indirectly criticizing France. Voltaire got into serious trouble for doing this.

This fictional Byzantium of the Enlightenment entrenched misconceptions and a distorted image of the civilization as a whole. Now, some of its claims did not make sense on the face of them, such as the idea of a decline that lasted 1,123 years, or that Byzantium was a servile despotism when, as both Montesquieu and Hegel admitted, emperors were frequently deposed. But there was a deeper cultural politics at work here. Enlightenment theory allowed Byzantium to be joined to the narrative of Roman history but only so long as it represented its long decline; it could be only a degenerate version of Rome, and the Byzantines themselves could never be true Romans (except in a few instances in Gibbon, when they manage to pull off a military feat worthy of the ancient Romans). Moreover, insofar as it was "Greek," Byzantium could only be a degenerate version of Greece, whose idealized ancient version became such an important component of European self-fashioning. Good ancient Greeks were conceptually separated from degenerate later Greeks, who had no civic virtue, spoke a vulgar and allegedly ungrammatical form of the language, did not care for classical antiquity, and practised an oriental form of superstitious Christianity. In sum, modern Europe was defining itself for the first time as a civilization based on the virtues of Greece, Rome, and Christianity, and it did so partly by stepping on the neck of the Byzantine tradition, which represented the bad versions of those three constituent elements.

Great Power Politics in the Nineteenth Century

The history of the Greeks took a dramatic turn in the early nineteenth century that precipitated wider changes in the perception of Byzantium. Indeed, the nineteenth century witnessed the biggest changes in western views of Byzantium since the ninth century, and again they stemmed from the politics of great empires. By the end of that century, Byzantium had generated an academic discipline of its own, featuring journals dedicated to it (*Byzantinische Zeitschrift* was founded first, by Karl Krumbacher, in 1892). It was also around this time that *positive* images of Byzantium began to gain a foothold in elite culture. But before we look at those, we must acknowledge a major transformation. Until roughly the middle of the nineteenth century, the dominant terminology remained the medieval one of "the empire of the Greeks" or "the empire of Constantinople." What we call Byzantium was still imagined as a phase in the continuous history of the Greek people, as an ethnic or national history, and it had been imagined that way in the West since ca. 800 AD. But by ca. 1900 that notion had been retired in the West and the Greek ethnic rubric was replaced by the abstract, artificial, and ethnically hollow term *Byzantium—Byzantine*, which was a minor term previously but is dominant today. Why did this shift happen and what were its consequences?

Within the course of just a few decades, history had conspired to make "the empire of the Greeks" a label that would trouble the minds of European statesmen. In 1821, the Christian inhabitants of Greece rose up against the Ottoman empire and finally secured recognition as the independent nation of the Greeks by 1828. This was a development to which the Great Powers acceded with reluctance. In the aftermath of the Napoleonic wars, their common approach was to safeguard the existing borders of their empires. This was especially true when it came to the so-called Eastern Question, which concerned the always-anticipated partition of the failing Ottoman empire. In this stand-off, every Christian power wanted to seize as much of the Ottoman empire as it could, but it also did not want its rivals to do so; as a result, their mutual watchfulness acted like the poles of a teepee that kept the Ottoman empire standing. But a single exception was made for Greece, in part because the widely advertised valour of the revolutionaries aroused romantic admiration by many Europeans. Philhellenism radically reversed the European stance that modern Greeks were unworthy of their ancestors. When they sought freedom from a cruel oriental despotism, Greeks were perceived as heroic again.

However, by the mid-nineteenth century those Greeks had begun to dream of empire, specifically of restoring "the empire of the Greeks" about which they read so much in western historiography. This plan was not at all to the liking of the Great Powers, where it was suspected that it was a Russian plot to use the Orthodox Greeks as proxies in a bid to seize Constantinople. That great journalist of the nineteenth century, Karl Marx, claimed as much in an editorial in the *New York Tribune* (March 29, 1854). Meanwhile, another German scholar, the bête noire of subsequent Greek historiography, Jakob Philipp Fallmerayer, argued in the 1830s that these so-called Greeks were not at all the descendants of Perikles but were superficially Hellenized Slavs and Albanians. Fallmerayer's thesis was also driven by Russophobia: support for these fake Greeks, he feared, was playing into the hands of the tsar. Matters came to a head in the Crimean War (1853–1856), when England and France joined forces to protect the Ottoman empire from Russian attack. Russophobia peaked in western Europe at this time, and one of its aspects was the idea that the tsar would use his Greek proxies to establish a new Orthodox empire at Constantinople (the origin of the term "jingoism" is from a ditty sung by the British during the war about how they would not let Russia take Constantinople). The Russian empire had long been tarred by association with Byzantium in western imagination (Napoleon had called tsar Alexander a "shifty Byzantine"). Moreover, Greece supported Russia in the Crimean War, sending units across the border to fight against the Turks (the Greeks lost). The leader of a Greek unit, the son of a hero of the Revolution, even proclaimed in print that his cause was "Greek Empire or Death!" This solidified the link between Greek irredentism and Russian imperialism. The British navy occupied Athens and seized the printing presses, as the newspapers had been printing the same slogan.

These developments tanked the stock of the "Greek empire" as a viable category in western historiography. By the end of the century, that category had effectively been replaced with the more sanitized and de-ethnicized "Byzantium," which provided a neutral space for international scholarly discussion. The Greek label was now too closely identified with the nationalism of the Greek state and its Grand Vision to restore the Greek Empire.

By contrast, this was not a problem in Greece itself. A brief digression is warranted on the reception of Byzantium in modern Greece. The success of the Revolution of 1821 was premised on persuading the European Powers that the revolutionaries were the descendants of the ancient Greeks who were seeking to restore their freedom through a heroic struggle against oriental despotism. This created an ideological imperative to stress continuity with antiquity, the Hellenic name, and the love of ancient monuments, even though many of the inhabitants of the new state were Romans and had not yet fully internalized their new Hellenic identity. At the same time, some leading intellectuals of the Greek Revolution were western-trained and therefore prejudiced against Byzantium, and so they did not want it to be included in the new national history, which jumped from antiquity to the present.

This narrative was soon problematized by Fallmerayer, who argued that there was no racial continuity between the ancient and the modern Greeks. It was largely in (outraged) reaction to this thesis that leading Greek historians, notably Konstantinos Paparrigopoulos (1815–1891), constructed a continuous longue durée history of the Hellenic nation, stretching from antiquity to the present, that *included* Byzantium. In one sense, this was easy to do, because all western histories written down to the mid-nineteenth century called Byzantium "the empire of the Greeks" and ethnicized its culture as Greek, even if in negative ways. Thus, Greek national historiography picked this narrative up and continued it at precisely the time that it was being discarded in the West (where it had been invented exactly one thousand years ago). However, the union of classical Greece, Byzantium, and the modern nation-state was a shotgun marriage that took place under the threat of Fallmerayer's race theory. It was done too hastily, confused racial and cultural categories, and left too many unresolved questions, including the incompatibility of Hellenism and Orthodoxy and the open secret of Byzantium's Roman identity. I am still regularly asked by Greeks whether Byzantine was "really" Greek—which is by far the issue that preoccupies them the most about it. This reveals that the national narrative has not fully stuck.

What did the invention of the category "Byzantium" entail for western historiography? Beyond facilitating the creation of a scholarly discipline, which was positive, the category had drawbacks. If the majority of the empire's population could not be regarded as Roman—which was still taboo—and they should not be regarded as ethnically Greek either, then who were they? This is the conundrum of politicized historiography, and it explains why scholars still stumble over this question. At least the medieval answer that they were *Graeci* reflected the truth that the Byzantines did, in their own minds, form an ethnic group distinct from others, both foreigners and many who were subjects of their empire (e.g., Slavs, Bulgarians, Vlachs, Armenians, etc.). In the face of this hole where Byzantine identity should be, scholars fell back upon Orthodoxy as the dominant identity of the empire and its population. Thus, twentieth-century scholarship on Byzantium became obsessed with Orthodoxy. Romanness continued to remain off limits and so did all discussions of ethnicity, as it is still widely (and incorrectly) assumed that

Orthodoxy erases ethnic differences. Byzantium was routinely called a multi-ethnic empire but no one dared to list these ethnicities in question. Some minority groups could be discussed (e.g., Jews, Armenians) because they had modern scholarly representatives to push their claims, but the broader discussion was effectively shut down, especially with Greek nationalists insisting that the majority population of Byzantium was "really" ethnically Greek regardless of what the sources said. This became a mine-field for western scholars, who generally avoided it in favour of an anachronistic image of Orthodox Ecumenism.

Meanwhile, many artists and novelists of the nineteenth century had built up a popular image of Byzantium as an exotic, oriental civilization, an image that is still with us, if in a less vulgar form. In France especially, this coincided with a general fin-de-siècle interest in decadence. Setting aside the novels and pseudo-histories of the period, Victorien Sardou's successful play *Théodora* (1884), staged as a Wagnerian monstrosity, highlighted the oriental decadence of Constantinople and contrasted it to the austere simplicity of classical Athens.[11] The twentieth-century scholarly obsession with Orthodoxy unfortunately played right into this set. For example, any Byzantine author (such as Prokopios of Kaisareia or Michael Psellos) who seemed to be engaging with ancient philosophy or was sceptical of miracles and the like was immediately assumed by scholars to be only superficially engaged with classical thought and pulled back into the ranks of the pious, on the ground that all Byzantines were supporters of theocracy, believed in holy men and miracles, and could never have used critical independent reason.[12] Modern scholars thereby perpetuated *Théodora*'s distinction

---

11 E. Boeck, "Archaeology of Decadence: Uncovering Byzantium in Victorien Sardou's *Theodora*," in *Byzantium/Modernism: The Byzantine as Method in Modernity*, ed. R. Betancourt and M. Taroutina (Leiden: Brill, 2015), 102–32.

12 For example, A. Cameron, *Procopius and the Sixth Century* (London: Duckworth, 1986).

between Athens and Constantinople. It was even asserted, and taken seriously by historians, that the Byzantines were unable to think about their society in secular terms at all, given that religion (prayers, icons, theocratic ideology, etc.) completely filled up their mental vision. In reality, this was yet another form of orientalism, precisely as defined by Edward Said (just replace Byzantines with Muslims or Arabs and you get the picture). In many of its forms, Byzantine Studies was a subspecies of orientalism, well into the twentieth century. Byzantium was exotic and deeply religious, even "spiritual," as no Byzantine could have a rational, secular thought.

These prejudices have been disastrous for the field of Byzantine Studies, especially as it concurrently drags along all the prejudices inherited from the deep medieval past. Even in the second half of the twentieth century it was possible for experts to publish denunciations of the worthlessness of Byzantine literature. A new element added to the mix was the growing (and by now ubiquitous) use of the adjective "Byzantine" to mean needlessly complicated, convoluted, intricate, or with a sinister ulterior motive. There is no sign that this lexical usage is abating: it appears regularly on television and in the movies. Moreover, some analysts even blamed Byzantium for the evils of the Soviet Union, seeing the Orthodox empire as the template and matrix of Soviet totalitarianism and ideological dogmatism. One historian published an article in a leading journal of the field saying that he could never have become a scholar of Byzantium as it reminded him too much of the Soviet Union.[13] Byzantium had once been imagined as Greek (i.e., fickle), then as a medieval version of the Ottoman empire (i.e., despotic), and later as the template for Soviet tyranny. More layers on the onion, all of them rotten.

---

13 A. Gurevich, "Why Am I Not a Byzantinist?," *Dumbarton Oaks Papers* 46 (1992): 89–96.

The Rehabilitation of Byzantium: Part of the Problem?

A contributor to the first edition of the *Cambridge Medieval History*, from 1923, stated that "in many ways the Byzantine was an Oriental," and yet, because John Bagnell Bury, classicist, Roman historian, and Regius professor at Cambridge, was the editor of the volume, its subtitle was "The Eastern Roman Empire (717–1453)."[14] Since then, the academic study of Byzantium has done much to counter this centuries-long accumulation of error and distortion, in most if not in all areas. This is only to be expected, as the search for facts and the truth had to correct images that were devised for now-obsolete political reasons. It is now possible to obtain fairly accurate information, or at least balanced debates grounded in the evidence, about many aspects of the culture. A great deal of scholarship in the field is first rate. Sometimes, however, the rehabilitation of Byzantium goes too far. For example, the rejection of the paradigm of decline leads some scholars to devise euphemisms and evasions for those periods when the empire was manifestly in decline (such as the 1070s, the late twelfth century, and much of the Palaiologan period). Change, flux, fluidity, diversity, originality, and other words that sound good to late modern liberal audiences are asserted primly at every turn, sometimes at the expense of the conservative continuity that marked the culture from start to finish. Some well-meaning attempts to make Byzantium fascinating by emphasizing its religious exotica or the palace intrigues of eunuchs and empresses veer close to the orientalist clichés and uncritical romances of the nineteenth century.

Western audiences might again be seeing themselves in the mirror here, or the inverted image of modernity that they have come to expect of any exotic "Other." Orthodoxy, especially its monastic versions, has long appealed to some

---

14 C. Diehl in J. B. Bury, ed., *The Cambridge Medieval History*, vol. 4: *The Eastern Roman Empire (717–1453)* (Cambridge: Cambridge University Press, 1923), 774.

discriminating westerners as a more authentic and spiritual form of Christianity. The nineteenth-century revival of interest in medieval art had its Byzantine side: Byzantine art was perceived as a more "spiritual" alternative to the supposedly oppressive classicizing aesthetic that was promoted by the modern nation-states, sometimes with a heavy hand. Icons were viewed as more mystical and less linear or rational. In the early twentieth century, Byzantine art was viewed by some through the prism of a bohemian avant-garde that oddly engaged with alternative modern sexualities—I say oddly because classical Greece was, to put it mildly, far more receptive to alternative sexualities than Byzantium. But such are the strange byways of reception.[15]

Many successful exhibitions of Byzantine art in recent decades have also traded on its image as "spiritual" and "mystical," a neo-Romantic marketing ploy that posits Byzantium as "An Age of Faith," a mystical alternative to the drab disappointments of modernity, our "iron cage" of technocratic disenchantment. This image, while successful for the museums involved, comes close to pitching an orientalist variant of uplifting medievalism. Most of Byzantine life was also drab and banal, enmeshed in bureaucracy and typical money-power rackets. That bastion of Orthodox spirituality, Mt. Athos, was effectively a religious theme park, and what made it succeed in the long term was that it manoeuvred politically to become very wealthy. Some Byzantine monasteries were tax shelters.

The next chapter will offer some thoughts about how Byzantium can be integrated into broader conceptions of history and how it might be promoted as good-for-thinking-with among people interested in history generally. I will here make two suggestions about where scholarship on Byzantium can grow. Much has already been done to rehabilitate it as a historical civilization, especially about how it "had its act

---

15 K. Kourelis, "Byzantium and the Avant-Garde: Excavation at Corinth, 1920s–1930s," *Hesperia* 76 (2007): 391–442.

together" as an organizational structure designed to withstand the shocks of history, or recover from them. But too much remains mired in confusion, and to clear it up we need to cut straight to the heart of the onion. Specifically, we have to heal the original sin of Roman denialism. So many aspects of Byzantium suddenly make so much more sense when we take its Romanness seriously, for example the Roman ethnic identity of its population, which fundamentally shaped how they interacted with other peoples, both inside and outside the empire. It also shaped their institutions, view of history, and the basis of their social cohesion.

A second imperative is that we must do a better job of communicating the virtues of Byzantine literature, a large, varied, and culturally coherent corpus. It is true that we have overcome past prejudices that condemned this literature as worthless, and we have made great strides toward understanding the rhetorical and stylistic templates that shaped it. But the current tendency among scholars to mostly redescribe texts through the technical rubrics and jargon of sociological theory does not help us promote its virtues among the general public, for all that it may be good for getting grants. Instead, we must find ways to communicate to people outside our field, in accessible terms, why Byzantine texts are interesting or enjoyable. To be sure, these texts will likely not become part of a World Literature curriculum. But with the exception of a few histories (Eusebios, Prokopios, Psellos, and Anna Komnene) and some monastic advice-literature, only specialists now read Byzantine texts, so there is at any rate much room for growth.

Chapter 2

Thinking Historically with Byzantium

> Ludwig Wittgenstein once asked, "Why do people say it is more logical to think that the sun revolves around the earth than that the earth rotates around its own axis?" "Because it appears as if the sun revolves around the earth." "Good," he said, "but how would it have appeared if the earth rotates around its own axis?"
>
> *Possibly apocryphal anecdote (simplified)*

How can Byzantium become compelling and relevant to broader audiences of readers interested in history, albeit without pandering to past stereotypes about its spirituality, mysticism, decadence, and decline? How can non-experts be persuaded to look its way more often? How might it be ensconced in broader debates about premodern history?

Byzantinists reasonably complain about these stereotypes and about the absence of Byzantium from broader public debates. Yet complaint might still be premature. Compared to classicists and medievalists, the field of Byzantine Studies has invested little in studying its own origins and ideologies, the history of western perceptions of Byzantium, and the politics of the stereotypes against which we are now protesting. Doing so would provide greater clarity and focus to our strategies of rehabilitation, and would also reveal how we remain complicit in perpetuating some problems, for instance the cognitive dissonance that is Roman denialism, or the trading on "mysticism" to sell tickets to a bourgeoisie eager to consume the Other.

Moreover, when it comes to the relative absence of Byzantium from the public consciousness, complaining about it is not enough. What positive reasons can we offer for its inclusion? Why should the general reading public or history enthusiasts care more about Byzantium and turn to it when thinking about the past and present? The insistence that all historical eras and cultures deserve attention won't fly even within academia, and is dead in the water outside it. Attention has to be earned. Some popularizing books do highlight the many achievements of Byzantium. This is necessary, but usually presupposes that one already finds the topic interesting. And many of these books treat Byzantium as important primarily for its services to the West (for example, blocking the Arabs from Europe and preserving classical Greek literature), or its services to Orthodox countries (e.g., for converting some Slavs), rather than for its own sake.

To be sure, while Byzantium will never rival ancient Greece and Rome in contemporary relevance, it will also never find itself in the marginal position of, say, Assyriology. There are many countries whose national history passes directly or tangentially through it and they have a stake in studying it and even making it a point of reference, whether they respect its history on its own terms or not. And the world's Orthodox Churches also have a stake in the theological, ecclesiastical, canonical, and artistic–architectural components of Byzantine civilization, which lay at the foundation of all Christian history, not just its Orthodox strand. Still, nations and Churches are likely to have ideological or utilitarian goals in their study of Byzantium, and they too will seek to appropriate it for their own purposes rather than to make it broadly relevant to the thinking of others. We come back, then, to the original dilemma: why *should* Byzantium be of general historical interest, apart from reasons stemming from religious confession or nationality? I do not mean to exclude those two reasons for studying it. They are both important and legitimate. But can we reach a less self-interested audience?

One problem that we face is a mismatch between expertise and market demand. What we want is to match what Byzantium has to offer with what people generally want to learn, yet experts rarely know what that is. We may have the bow but we can't see the target in the mist. This chapter will suggest some new targets.

As we seek ways to make Byzantium relevant, there is a precious resource that we have not yet tapped: the intellectual trajectories that led each Byzantinist to this field. No one is born a Byzantinist, and I doubt that anyone wanted to become one from an early age, yet somehow during our teenage or young adult years each of us ended up here, as a result of decisions made in the course of a personal and intellectual narrative. Let us set aside the inscrutable depths of personal psychology, whose exploration would require a psychologist or psychoanalyst, though they certainly played their part. We can all tell a more surface story about how we began with questions that any thinking person might ask about history and ended up studying, say, ninth-century saints' lives. Indeed, I am increasingly curious to ask my colleagues, "Why on earth did you decide to become a *Byzantinist*?" (or, sometimes, "Why did *you* decide that?").

In this spirit, I will give a *very* brief account of the trajectory that led me here. Its only redeeming quality is that it reveals some of the general questions that might lead a person to this field who, at the start of the story, can reasonably be described as "the very opposite of a Byzantinist." Those questions still shape my research, although they have mutated in unexpected ways; moreover, as I have become less ambitious in my thinking, what used to be means have become ends.

In school (in Greece), I chose to specialize in biology and physics, which I declared as my majors when I came to college in the US. Until that time, I had no interest in history, literature, or language, which in Greece were taught in a whiny nationalist way that reeked of moldy institutions and insecurities and induced little more than boredom. I was especially indifferent toward the study of ancient Greek, which I regarded as the most useless thing in the world. And yet, in my last year in high school, I realized that science could not answer (or really even address) some of the most fundamental questions about human beings as I experienced them in daily and political life. I turned to Machiavelli and Nietzsche, precisely because they were designated in our official textbooks as the most wrong and evil (not coincidentally, they were the first and last modern philosopher, respectively). Upon reading them, I saw that both were laying down ground-rules for "modernity" by strategically appropriating, rejecting, and distorting aspects of ancient Greece, Rome, and early Christianity, in various combinations.

The philosophical issues eventually grew so large that I had to go back to those original sources: out of what materials exactly had modern subjects, myself included, been constituted? By this point I was in college, majoring in physics and biology. But thanks to the open format of the American college system, I was able to find professors with whom I could talk about these issues. I swallowed a big pill of irony when I began to relearn ancient Greek (and Latin) and switched my majors to philosophy and history. My new focus was on Homer and Plato, Roman state-formation, and New Testament scholarship and Patristics, and the goal was to understand their role in the making of modernity.

The next twist in the story came when I soon realized that there was only one civilization in the whole of history that fused these three components together in something resembling their original forms, namely a civilization that was Greek-speaking and so accessed and preserved ancient Greek thought and literature in their original language; that was a Roman society in terms of its state institutions, ideology, and genealogy, and also in the national or ethnic identity of the majority of its inhabitants; and that was also a Christian society whose social and personal values were ostensibly derived from the Greek Bible and whose official doctrines and religious organization were defined by the first Church Councils. That one society was Byzantium. The most quintessentially classical texts and the founding thinkers of western modernity had led me straight to it.

This conclusion was paradoxical, for most narratives about the rise and history of the West relegate Byzantium to an undefined eastern or marginal space that lies outside Europe proper. The concept of "the West" is, of course, a modern invention and problematic in many ways. It bears some genealogical relation to the idea of Christendom (an early modern notion conceived in opposition to Islam) and to that of Europe (which poses as a continent but plainly is not, as any map makes clear). The concept of the West was a twentieth-century effort to impute a general sense of cultural unity to the predominantly white countries on "this" side of the Iron Curtain. Samuel Huntington, a former Pentagon analyst and Cold Warrior trained to view history as *The Clash of Civilizations* (1996), conceded that Islamic and Orthodox cultures had also inherited some aspects of classical civilization but not to the same degree that "the West" had. He lumped modern Greece and Russia into the non-western "Orthodox" category as "an offspring of Byzantine civilization." This is a standard conservative view. While I was writing these words I was also reading Walter Scheidel's study of wealth inequality throughout history, and he directly states that Byzantium was not a part of Europe proper.[1]

But hold on. Few attempts to define the modern West are crass or honest enough to admit that it consists of a handful of wealthy countries in northwestern Europe, their north American patron, and their armies (NATO). Most attempts instead postulate a cultural genealogy, defining the West as those countries that have ancient Greece, Rome, and Christianity in their cultural DNA (i.e., "Plato to NATO"). But by this definition, Byzantium was the most western of all cultures that have ever existed.

---

[1] S. Huntington, *The Clash of Civilizations and the Remaking of World Order* (New York: Simon & Schuster, 1996), 69–70, 139; W. Scheidel, *The Great Leveler: Violence and the History of Inequality from the Stone Age to the Twenty-First Century* (Princeton: Princeton University Press, 2017), 90. For a different approach, see K. A. Appiah, "There Is No Such Thing as Western Civilisation," *The Guardian*, November 9, 2016, available at www.theguardian.com/world/2016/nov/09/western-civilisation-appiah-reith-lecture.

Just to be clear: this is not a pitch that Byzantium should be included in the privileged western club, which is not exactly a badge of honour and prestige, though it comes with definite advantages. The point is rather that cultural definitions of the West yield only selective results, because they are reverse-engineered to produce the desired outcome: northwestern Europe, defined ostensibly not by its arms and industry but its alleged cultural genealogy. If we apply these ostensible cultural definitions more rigorously and thereby draw more attention to Byzantium in the West, so much the better. And it would be even better still if we realized that other cultures too that have been traditionally excluded from the charmed club of the West also share aspects of the same DNA, including Islamic cultures. This might provide a basis for bridge-building once petroleum and racism cease to dominate the terms of the discussion. A leading scholar of the Arabic reception of ancient Greek thought, Dimitri Gutas (emeritus at Yale), refers to the "West" in this field of study as encompassing everything west of the Indus river. We will later find more reasons to study this whole area (Iran to Ireland) as a unit (whether we want to use that tricky term for it or not).

My second realization was that Greek, Roman, and Christian elements coexisted in Byzantium in a state of tension, both creative and destructive. This was poorly reflected in the scholarship, if at all. The Roman element was at best viewed as an empty shell or a purely formal aspect of the culture, but often it was just dismissed. Then, the classical Greek and Orthodox Christian elements were assumed to have arrived at a point of happy synthesis, as a unified ideology that constituted the culture's perfectly integrated (Christian) mentality. But the sources do not present such a picture. What we find there instead is the robust presence of all three elements in a state of fascinating tension that drew me in.

Consider the axis Hellenism–Christianity. Far from the two being at peace or achieving some sort of "natural" symbiosis, some early Christian leaders left no doubts that they basically wanted to exterminate Hellenism altogether, everything but the language itself. Once their party took over the Roman empire, however, and became its official religion, they accomplished this only to a limited degree, for example by abolishing or ceasing to attend Greek religion, festivals, games, and other aspects of the culture. They also stigmatized the name "Hellene" by causing it to mean "pagan." This resulted in the paradox of Arab, Persian, and Chinese non-Christians being called "Hellenes" by Greek-speaking Christians. The Persians had once been the enemies of the Greeks, but now they *were* "the Hellenes." Yet not all Christians were zealots in this mold, and accommodations became possible. For example, understanding Orthodox theology required some knowledge of ancient philosophy, which was of course selectively interpreted, but at least this meant that it had to be partially preserved, while secular elites retained their prestige literary culture, such as Homer, Plato, and Demosthenes. Thus the basic educational system of elite culture did not change much from antiquity. A great deal of Greek thought and literature thereby survived through the Byzantine millennium. To give another example from architecture, the Parthenon in Athens was converted into a church of the Virgin that was famous as a Christian shrine but never shed the glory of its Greek past in the eyes of Christian beholders. Even its architecture was not much changed. Still, some worried about its past pagan associations. Thus, it was simultaneously a survival, a transformation, and site of tension.

Byzantine culture never dropped its guard against the temptations of Hellenism. The fear of a new Julian—the last emperor to champion a pagan version of Hellenism and attack Christianity (361–363)—never abated. Byzantine intellectuals often accused each other of being "new Julians," and philosophical paganism was suspected behind many new ideas. This was reasonable, for quite a few Byzantine thinkers did in fact flirt with non-Christian or even anti-Christian notions. The intellectual culture was thus hardly monolithic, though Orthodoxy was certainly not a welcoming environment for new ideas. In fact, during the Renaissance the West received a potent dose of Hellenic pagan thought from the last great Byzantine philosopher, Georgios Gemistos Plethon, a Platonist. The Hellenic and the Orthodox traditions sat uneasily beside each other in Byzantium, just as they have in modern European thought from the Renaissance on through the Enlightenment and postmodernity.

Consider also the Greek–Roman axis. Here we observe one of the most fascinating instances of cross-hybridization in history, and we can observe it *only* in the case of Byzantium. The Roman ethnonym and identity drove out any sense of Greek ethnicity from the Greek-speaking inhabitants of formerly Greek lands, a transformation that was accelerated by the polemical religious sense given to the word *Hellenism* by the Church. The subjects of the empire—whether high or low in social class, and whether provincial or in Constantinople—identified collectively as Romans (*Romaioi*). Thus, the long relationship in antiquity between Greece and Rome was finally resolved in favour of Greek Romanness, in a way that no classicist would ever have predicted (classicists rarely look past the third century). What Byzantium proves is that ancient Romanization ultimately prevailed, and it won a far bigger victory in the Greek-speaking east than it did in western Europe, where it eventually went extinct after the barbarian invasions. The Greeks became the staunchest Romans. In Byzantium, they traced the history of their polity and society back to Rome in Italy and then, via Aeneas, to Troy. Their capital was at Constantinople, or New Rome, not far from Troy, and their state, court, titles, offices, laws, courts, armies, and political ideology were derived directly from the ancient Roman empire, as was a considerable amount of their vocabulary for daily life. A strong case can be made that this was a Roman society not only because it believed itself to be that but because its fundamental templates were Roman. This Greek-speaking Roman nation persevered for centuries under Ottoman rule after 1453 AD, keeping its name and identity largely intact.

On the other hand, the Latin language lapsed in Byzantium around 600 AD, so what emerged after that was a Greek-speaking Roman society. This society did Roman things, but it did them in Greek. For example, it remembered its history through the Greek historians of Rome, not Latin ones.

Byzantium effectively was Rome translated into Greek. Imagine a United States of America, for example, in which everything is in Spanish, a language with its own distinguished literary and imperial past. To tweak this story, notions of Greek ethnicity resurfaced among certain Byzantine thinkers during the empire's last centuries. They happened under the intense pressure of conquest and colonization by western Europeans after the Fourth Crusade, who regarded themselves as the only legitimate Romans. Few Byzantines paid attention to these attempts at Greek ethnic revival at the time, but they laid the foundation for the rebirth of a Greek nation in the nineteenth century.

Consider finally the Roman–Christian axis. In many ways, this proved to be the most mutually reinforcing relationship. You would not have thought so before 311 AD, when the imperial authorities sought to eliminate Christianity for being antithetical to "the religion of the Romans." But the emperor Galerius (in 311) and then Constantine and Licinius (in 313) allowed Romans to be Christians, if they so chose. Religion was thereby dissociated from the legal and political identity of the subjects of the empire. Then, in 380 Theodosius I decreed that all his subjects had to adhere to his own Nicene version of Christianity or face various legal penalties and discrimination. Subsequent emperors reinforced that policy, with the effect that "the religion of the Romans" became the Catholic-Orthodox Christianity of the imperial Church. Religious and political identity were once again fused. This had dramatic consequences for the original Christian project to remake the world along Christian lines and sweep away all existing ethnicities and their traditional customs. When the Roman state co-opted the Church, these ambitions were tamed and drastically curtailed. Roman secular society, with most of its laws, procedures, social values, economic structures, and habits of thought, continued on without much change, experiencing only gradual Christian influence.

Byzantine political ideology also operated henceforth along two distinct and parallel lines, one theocratic (articulated by bishops such as Eusebios of Kaisareia), according to which God appointed the emperor to rule, and a second one derived from the Roman national consensus that emperors had long employed to justify their position in the eyes of the *res publica Romana*: according to this view, the emperor of the Romans derived his legitimacy directly from the Roman people, for example through mass rituals of acclamation, and defined his role as a servant of the national interest of the Roman *populus*. There were many other ways, which remain unexplored, in which ancient Roman conceptions of religion shaped Byzantine practice, for example in how the Byzantines honoured the emperor as a quasi-god. These make theologians uncomfortable, but were real nonetheless in Byzantine society. All this existed at the intersection of Roman and Christian elements of the culture.

Not all aspects of Byzantine life were marked by cultural tensions. Some were rather the product of confluence, as Greek, Roman, and Christian elements came together to produce something unique that would never have existed in that form without all three. Some of these products were heavy hitters in world history. For example, to take *institutions* first, in his brilliant book on *The Birth of the Hospital in the Byzantine Empire* Tim Miller showed how the institution of the hospital was created through the combination of Christian charity, philanthropy, and service, with Greek scientific medicine and the institutional organization and funding structures made possible by the later Roman imperial state in its concern for the wellbeing of its subjects.[2] Or consider *monuments*: the cathedral of Hagia Sophia, the most amazing church ever built, was the culmination of centuries of Roman imperial architecture and was designed, by engineers educated in pagan-Hellenic schools, to embody a Christianized Neoplatonic philosophy of divine light. Its architects were pagan Neoplatonists.[3] How about *texts*? The Acts of the Church Councils contain records made according to Roman

---

2 T. Miller, *The Birth of the Hospital in the Byzantine Empire*, 2nd ed. (Baltimore: Johns Hopkins University Press, 1997).

3 A. Kaldellis, "The Making of Hagia Sophia and the Last Pagans of

notarial protocol that reflect debates over Greek philosophical terms and their implications for Christian theology. Even single *words* spanned the spectrum. The term *politeia*, for instance, had a deep philosophical pedigree (e.g., as the title of Plato's *Republic*), though in Byzantium it was frequently a vessel for the distinctively Roman idea of the *res publica*, while in Christian contexts it could refer to a saint's way of life.

Consider also evocative *moments*. One of the most solemn moments in Byzantine history occurred when the longest-reigning emperor of the Romans, Basileios II (976–1025), mounted the Acropolis in Athens in 1018 to celebrate a military triumph in the Parthenon, a temple to the Virgin Mary. Or consider how the most clever Byzantine, Michael Psellos (eleventh century), explained that the inscription on Jesus' cross was carved in the three languages that represented the basic elements of his own culture: Latin stood for practical excellence and political strength, as the Romans were the most energetic and powerful nation; Greek stood for the study of nature, as the Greeks surpassed all others in their knowledge of the nature of beings; and Hebrew stood for infallible theology, as the Jews were the first to understand God. This reading of the inscription on the Cross had originally been proposed by Cyril, the bishop of Alexandria in the early fifth century, proving that this tripartite reading resonated with Byzantines across the centuries.[4]

This schematic mode of analysis works for *individuals* too. Synesios, a man with a wicked wit, was the bishop of Kyrene in the early fifth century. He claimed to be descended from Herakles (as Kyrene, in north Africa, was settled by Spartans from Thera); he defended his possession of "Hellenic" learning; and was a pagan Neoplatonist at heart. He agreed to

---

New Rome," *Journal of Late Antiquity* 6 (2014): 347–66.

4 Michael Psellos, *Oration on the Crucifixion of Our Lord Jesus Christ* 2, lines 359–78; ed. E. Fisher, *Michaelis Pselli orationes hagiographicae* (Stuttgart: Teubner, 1994), 174–75. Cf. Cyril of Alexandria, *Commentary on Luke*, ed. J.-P. Migne, *Patrologiae Cursus Completus Series Graeca*, 161 vols. (Paris: Migne, 1857–66), 72:col. 937.

be bishop only on the condition that he could stay married to his wife and not have to literally believe in the Christian doctrines such as Resurrection. He also wrote, from a nationalist Roman point of view, a treatise *On Kingship* that argued against giving foreigners positions in the army and state and that influenced subsequent Byzantine political thought. However, not everyone was as versatile as Synesios. Some Byzantines "specialized" in one of these aspects of their culture, either in religion, by renouncing all "Greek" wisdom and secular worldly ties and travelling the world along monastic networks; or in careers that were distinctive to Romans, such as statecraft and war (they might be overheard saying that they paid little attention to Christian things); or in classical learning, in which case they might (in later times) call themselves Hellenes, which gradually came to mean learned gentlemen. Saints, classical scholars, and generals and politicians were three distinctly different types of person produced by this culture: they represented different corners of its value-system, and managed to coexist.

It is fascinating to trace these permutations and combinations which can be studied nowhere else as clearly as in the case of Byzantium. Moreover, they involve elements that are familiar to students of the classics and of "western" tradition generally: one simply has to follow them into the next stage of their evolution without assuming that it necessarily has to be geographically situated in western Europe. This is one of the main limitations of so many grand narratives of big classical themes which jump directly from antiquity to the Renaissance and then to the modern nation-states, assuming that this is the only or the most interesting pathway of cultural genealogy. The exclusion of Byzantium from these narratives is purely ideological and can be explained sufficiently by the prejudices and stereotypes exposed in the previous chapter. After all, studying Byzantium involves no "exotic" new elements that might put one off and requires no new languages, at least for those who have a classical education (and for those who don't there is now an abundance of translated material).

This, then, is one way in which Byzantium is good to think with, at least for those who want to stay within an otherwise mainstream "western" context. It is a laboratory for the study of Greek, Roman, and Christian culture as it was the only society in history that combined them in their original ancient forms, giving rise to distinctive tensions and permutations. The approach is admittedly schematic, but that is precisely what makes it good to think with and able to draw in outsiders. To tell them that it was monolithically Orthodox, which the field has been doing for a long time, is to flatten it to one dimension and diminish its broad appeal, whereas to tell them that it was infinitely complex and nuanced (the opposite extreme to which younger scholars are increasingly attracted) is to offer nothing at all. At the end of analysis, infinite complexity makes speech impossible.

While learning to read Byzantine culture in this way, I put the philosophical problems of modernity on the backburner. I was enthralled by the spectacular vistas that Byzantium offered from its commanding position at the crossroads of history, and the breathtaking scale of it all. Byzantine civilization began when there were still some people who could read and write in Egyptian hieroglyphics; the oracle of Delphi and the Olympic games were still in existence; and the main god of worship in the east was Zeus. When Byzantium ended, the world had cannons and printing presses, and some people who witnessed the fall of Constantinople in 1453 lived to hear about Columbus' journey to the New World. Chronologically, Byzantium spans the entire arc from antiquity to the early modern period, and its story is intertwined with that of all the major players in world history on this side of the Indus river: Greeks, Romans, Jews, Goths, Franks, Persians, Arabs, Lombards, Avars, Bulgars, Slavs, Vikings, the Rus', Armenians, Pechenegs, Turks, Normans, and Mongols, to name a few with their conventional names. Byzantium lasted for so long that it outlived many of its own "heirs," such as most of the post-Roman barbarian kingdoms in the west, the Umayyad and Abbasid caliphates, the Seljuk sultanate, the Crusader states, and so on. In fact, Byzantium is possibly the only (but is certainly the best) connecting thread among all these intertwined stories, as Edward Gibbon realized when he reached the later phases of his history of the decline of Rome. He did not at that point focus much on the internal history of Byzantium itself; instead, he used its vicissitudes to orient the stories of those other peoples around it into a coherent narrative. Byzantium provided an excellent vantage point from which to recount and connect much of world history. It is perhaps not an accident that the best historian of the Enlightenment, who was also one of the first and most ambitious "world historians," chose Byzantium as his through-line. Byzantium can play that role again.

I sometimes tell my students that Byzantium is "the empire of the middle ground," because chronologically it spans the era between antiquity and modernity and also because geographically it sat astride Europe and Asia, directly between what would become Christian Europe and the Islamic world. At first, Byzantium straddled three continents by itself, then two (after the seventh century), and finally it was limited to just one (after the fourteenth). It was right in the middle of things as the most important developments in history were taking place, to say nothing of those important developments for which it itself was directly responsible, such as the codification and institutionalization of both the Christian and Roman orders, and the preservation and shaping of the classical Greek legacy.

Consider the benefits that the field would reap from a concerted campaign to have "Byzantium" fully recognized as an integral and indispensable part of "a long Roman history." The forum where this has happened most intensively so far is among war-gamers, both online and table-top, though this debate remains invisible to most scholars; it was entirely by accident that I was informed it was happening. A more concerted campaign to include Byzantium in Roman history could be promoted by scholars, journalists, and creators of popular media as well as by textbooks, introductory college courses, and other venues of popular history. It would bring greater visibility and weight to Byzantium (as the eastern Roman empire) in the public eye. To be sure, it would require that basic notions about Roman history be adjusted, especially among denialist historians, but it would be a significant victory for the field and would surely redound to Byzantium's public advantage.

Ancient historians are already exploring the ways in which Rome was a diverse and evolving civilization, and how Romanness never meant only one thing. Now is the perfect time to persuade them that they, and the public at large, should expand the scope of this civilization to include its direct descendant in the east, the society that called itself Romanía. The history of Rome can be reimagined as a gradual process of imperial expansion and civic consolidation, resulting, by 400 AD, in a fairly homogeneous Christian Roman world. Its potential in the West was broken and scattered by the barbarian invasions, while its history in the Near East was cut short by the Arab conquests and subsequent mass conversion to Islam. The Roman nation survived these historical bottlenecks in only one place, Byzantium–Romanía, where it went on to flourish for a thousand more years. And the Roman ethnicity survived under the Ottoman empire as well. I find such a long-term view of Roman history fascinating. Do we have the nerve to entertain such an expansive vista?

In my experience, it is Byzantinists themselves who pose the biggest obstacle here. Unfortunately, many are still trapped in Roman denialism and bristle or scoff at the notion that we accept the Byzantines' claim to be Romans. They prefer to dismiss this claim as deceptive or delusional and stick to religion as the only or main interpretive axis. Scholars from neighbouring fields (Classics, Near Eastern Studies, Slavic Studies, and some medievalists) are far more receptive to a Roman Byzantium. And I mean Roman in essence, not just in name. Labels are important, but so are the narratives that sustain them. It is from stories that identities derive their essence, and the narrative of Byzantium is a Roman one as well as a Christian one. That may put it on a bigger map. In finding itself again, Romanía can change our understanding of Roman history broadly.

We should think Big, in bigger terms even than the 1,123 years that elapsed between the foundation and conquest of

Constantinople. Let's try to think even bigger, remembering that "Byzantium" was invented through an attempt to pare history down to a manageable size, by postulating that one phase of the Roman empire was "essentially" different from the others, thereby cutting Roman history into smaller bits. Other than scholarly convenience, there is no good reason to do this. There was only ever one Roman *res publica*. It began as a city on the Tiber in Italy, expanded to encompass a huge empire, and, in the process, it became an idea: the city had become a world, to which the name Romanía was given by the fourth century AD. Over many centuries, this idea turned the Greeks into Romans and established a branch-office of its capital among them. This eastern version of Rome and the Romans survived the fall of the western empire in the fifth century and the Arab conquests in the seventh century, and endured until the fifteenth century. In sum, we are talking about a coherent history that lasted over two thousand years. The core of it was the (expanding and movable) community of the Roman people, as well as the idea and single polity that held them together. It is possible to extend this history into Ottoman times, as its Roman subjects retained their ethnic identity as a distinct group that remembered their former independence and imperial glory. It was not until the nineteenth century that this idea was finally scattered, replaced in Greece, for example, by a notion of Greek nationality. The history of the Roman people stretches, with no major discontinuities albeit with many gradual changes, from Romulus to the end of the Ottoman empire.

The continuity between Rome and New Rome is a striking version of the philosophical paradox of Theseus' ship (Plutarch, *Life of Theseus* 23.1). If a ship replaces every one of its components as it is gradually restored and repaired, including (why not?) its crew, does it remain the same ship? Over the course of two thousand years, Rome shifted its physical location; changed its language from mostly Latin and some Greek to only Greek; changed its government from a monarchy to a republic and then a monarchy; changed its religion to Christian Orthodoxy; went from being a dominant empire to a subordinate client-kingdom; and took in so many new populations that the Romans at the end of the story were not related to those at the start except through their common identity as Romans, an identity, however, that they always felt keenly. All these were big changes, to be sure, but most of them took effect over centuries. The only one that represented a dramatic rupture in continuity, and was viewed as such by the Romans, was the switch from Republic to Empire, but this was also the only major change that had nothing to do with "Byzantium," as it happened over three centuries before the foundation of Constantinople. As for all the other changes, "Rome" had ample time to adjust to them without losing its coherence. I note for the record that vastly more discontinuous and haphazard states such as the "Holy Roman Empire" do receive the benefit of unified treatment. There were no major turning points in the history of Rome / New Rome that require us to invent new labels or essences. It was all one history. Is our historical vision broad enough for this conception?

In 1935, the Romanian historian Nicolae Iorga published a book called *Byzantium after Byzantium* on the political and cultural influence that Byzantium exerted after its fall on Wallachia and Moldavia.[5] The enticing concept in its title proved to be more successful than its actual contents, and has spawned a cottage industry of reception-studies: Byzantium had a long afterlife in some parts of the world. I have long thought that we could also use the complementary notion of a "Byzantium before Byzantium." This would be nothing less than what we now typically call the Roman empire. It displays traits that definitely point toward its Byzantine phase. Consider, for example, the second-century AD orator Ailios Aristeides (or Aelius Aristides), from western Asia Minor. Polymnia Athanassiadi has brilliantly shown how he was a proto-Byzantine figure.[6] Aristeides was one of the leading proponents of classical Greek culture and wrote a long and impressive speech in

---

5 N. Iorga, *Byzance après Byzance: Continuation de l'histoire de la vie byzantine* (Bucharest: Institut d'études byzantines, 1935).

6 P. Athanassiadi, *Vers la pensée unique: La montée de l'intolérance dans l'Antiquité tardive* (Paris: Belles Lettres, 2010).

praise of Athens' cultural achievements. He was also a Roman citizen (as is evident from his full name) and wrote a famous speech that praised Rome for remaking the world in its own image. His idealized image of Rome explains why elites from around the empire were becoming reconciled to the Roman order and were seeking to join it actively. Aristeides also worried constantly about his health and developed a close personal relationship with a healer god, Asklepios. He wrote an account of the various remedies that the god prescribed for his afflictions, the *Sacred Tales*, in which he recounts how the god appeared to him in one dream and gave him a special divine name, Theodoros (or Theodore). This complicated man, who occupied the intersection of Greek literary culture, Roman political identity, and a religion of personal salvation encoded in the name Theodore, was basically a Byzantine. It was no accident that his works became standard rhetorical texts in Byzantium, as he articulated fundamental aspects of its culture in the language of imperial Greek rhetoric.

But, one objects, isn't this teleology? Aren't we reading an earlier figure in light of later developments, as if we expect history to lead in that (and only that) direction? The answer is definitely No. Seeing Aristeides as a proto-Byzantine is not teleological because "Byzantium" was not a separate thing at all, it is only a modern way of labelling one phase in the long history of the Roman empire. But when did it begin? Every answer will be arbitrary to a degree. Conventionally, we say 324 or 330 AD, when Constantine inaugurated or founded Constantinople. But some historians can, with reason, point to 284, the accession of Diocletian, who began to reform the Roman state in ways that established the framework for early Byzantine history. Yet if we opt for a cultural rather than an institutional definition, we can push that further back, depending on what we are looking for. Things were beginning to look quite "Byzantine" already by the time of Aristeides, and even earlier. Consider the Jewish priest and historian Josephos (first century AD). He wrote long treatises in Greek defending the Old Testament from attacks against it by Greek gentiles, and he switched sides during the Jewish War to join the Romans, obtaining citizenship and a Roman name (Flavius, the same name that Constantine would later sport). As a Greek-writing Roman Biblical monotheist, Josephos was also a proto-Byzantine, for all that his background was so different from that of Ailios Aristeides. Each of them represented the different strands that were coming together and coalescing to form a distinctively Byzantine articulation. Indeed, the only people who cared for the works of Josephos originally appear to have been the Christians and later the Byzantines, who treated him as an honorary Christian apologist and writer.

"Byzantium," in other words, was a distinctive constellation that formed in the spaces between Roman Jews like Josephos, Roman Greeks like Aristeides, and Hellenized Romans like the emperors Hadrian (117–138) and Marcus Aurelius (161–180). In this sense Byzantium emerged long before Diocletian or Constantine. Its prehistory included ideas about the portability of Rome ("Rome is wherever the emperor is," a general told the emperor Commodus in 193),[7] the recurring fear that an emperor would move the capital to the east (said of Caesar and Caligula), and the possibility that the empire would be formally divided between a western and eastern half (this was foreshadowed already by its division between Octavian and Marcus Antonius, and proposed again in 193 AD and 211 AD before becoming a permanent reality in 395 AD). These were not mere signs or omens of things to come: they were fully Byzantine developments already underway in the early empire, embedded in the core dynamics of Roman history. "Byzantium" was a process taking place within the empire long before Constantine.

Such a proactive Byzantine concept can thereby colonize earlier Roman history, an idea that is both fun and illuminating to think with. Instead of asking ancient Roman historians for kind permission to enter the Roman club, we can make a far more ambitious claim, namely that Byzantium accounts for the majority of Roman historian, especially if we add to it the ethnic *Romaioi* or *Romioi* of the Ottoman empire.

---

7 Pompeianus in Herodian, *History of Events after Marcus Aurelius* 1.6.5.

Another long history into which Byzantium can be slotted is that of the Greek language and its literature. Indeed, there are few languages that deliver as much bang for your buck as ancient Greek. Once you learn to read it, over two thousand years of Greek writing open up before you. You need to make only minor adjustments to read its later koine ("common") forms. All languages change over time, but Greek may be the language that has changed the least in the three thousand years of its recorded history, and especially so between the fifth century BC and the fifteenth century AD, during which period its written forms remained fairly conservative. There is much that historical linguistics can tell us about how and why Byzantine society played such a stabilizing role in the history of the Greek language. To be sure, a divergence between the spoken vernacular and the high-register written forms of Greek had already appeared in Roman times, i.e., in proto-Byzantium, but these different forms always remained in close contact with each other. For a classicist, the effort required to learn vernacular Greek is about the same as that required for a native speaker of modern English to learn Old English, i.e., a semester or two of college-level study. In sum, with relatively small effort all phases of the history of Greek are made accessible. Byzantium thereby fits into another Big Picture, and occupies a huge portion of it.

Unfortunately, few make that effort. I continue to be baffled by classicists who learn this amazing language and then spend their careers reading only a few texts that are clustered together in the fifth and fourth centuries BC and the first and second centuries AD, when there exist so many other fascinating and profound as well as weird and funny texts, written in the same language, to be had from the next thousand years as well. There is no reason to dwell here on the biases that produce this odd behaviour with its lopsided results, such as dozens of dissertations each year on Homer, all desperate to say something new, and zero dissertations on Theodoros Prodromos, the witty philosopher–satirist of the twelfth century AD, or his contemporary Ioannes Tzetzes, a classical scholar whom many classicists will encounter at some point in their research. Now, I freely grant that the thought of some classical authors, Plato for example, is more important and worth engaging with than anything that Byzantium produced. But understanding the philosophy of Plato (or Thucydides or ...) is not what the overwhelming majority of classicists do these days. They are engaged in cultural study and literary analysis of the sort that can be applied to almost any period of recorded history. (We will return to this problem at the end of Chapter 3.)

Byzantium marks no rupture in the history of Greek literature. There was no discernable break or new start in language or literature to match the foundation of Constantinople. Christian literature had already begun before that and pagan literature continued to be produced long after it, even assuming that religion was some kind of divider. In general, literary production continued more or less as before, affected naturally by the ups and downs of history. The tradition of Greek rhetoric, for example, flew past the alleged transition from Rome to Byzantium, without skipping a beat. So did the tradition of Greek historiography, running from Herodotos to Kritoboulos of Imbros in the fifteenth century AD and beyond. Not surprisingly, it is a Byzantinist (Leonora Neville, a contributor to this series) who has proposed anew to survey the whole of Greek historiography without respecting artificial labels that get in the way of our seeing it in its totality.[8]

Byzantine literature was thus only a phase in the ongoing story of Greek literature, and it evolved gradually from what came before, becoming more Roman and more Christian over time. But just as we did with periodization, we can extend the rubric of Byzantine literature backward in time too. Following the biographer Philostratos (ca. 235 AD), classicists use the label "Second Sophistic" to refer to the Greek literature of the second and third centuries AD. This period includes Dio Chrysostom, Aristeides, Plutarch, the romance novels, Arrian, Lucian, Galen, Athenaios, and many other authors. We could

---

8 L. Neville, *Guide to Byzantine Historical Writing* (Cambridge: Cambridge University Press, 2018).

just as well call it proto-Byzantine: not only did it set the stage for Byzantine literature proper, the Byzantines chose to preserve huge amounts of it precisely because they knew that it laid the foundation of much of their own literary culture, more so perhaps than did the literature of classical antiquity. The literature of the Second Sophistic recast many classical themes in terms that catered to a Greek-speaking society under Roman rule. This is after all what Byzantium was, and so it favoured the preservation of this body of writings.

These remarks are offered less as a thesis or argument about history and more as an invitation to view longer stretches of history from an overtly Byzantine perspective than are traditionally allotted to it. I do not expect that this perspective will be readily adopted by other fields, by textbooks, or in courses. Yet to glimpse history from that vantage point, even for a moment, is a valuable experience for it adds another voice to the conversation about the transition from antiquity to what came after it. One and the same period can be seen validly as early Christian, later Roman, early medieval, or early Byzantine, depending on the narrative at hand. But right now, one voice in the conversation—that belonging to "late antiquity"—has displaced the others, and Byzantium has been marginalized by it more than the others. In the past two generations, late antiquity has emerged as a self-proclaimed new field claiming jurisdiction over everything that happened between the later third and the eighth centuries, and between the Atlantic and Mesopotamia.

What is the relationship between late antiquity and Byzantium? For starters, both fields are modern inventions (originating, respectively, in the late nineteenth and late twentieth centuries), and their made-up names promote different ways of looking at their respective (but overlapping) slices of history. "Late antiquity" looks at a period that had always been of concern to European scholars, albeit previously it was dispersed among disciplines that did not communicate well with each other and, by the mid-twentieth century, were spinning in their tracks: the study of the later Roman empire was mired in debates over decline and fall and the origin of the modern European nations in the barbarian invasions; Patristics was stuck on dry theology and doctrine; Syriac and Sasanian Persian studies were marginalized and as yet underdeveloped; and the study of early Islam was beyond the pale for ancient historians. Late antiquity united these previously disparate fields by positing a single academic terrain in which they could coexist and share notes. It stretched geographically from the Roman and post-Roman West to Persia and the Islamic world, and chronologically from the third to the eighth centuries AD. Expanding like an empire of its own, it occupied the space in which "early Byzantium" used to be situated. Late antiquity shocked its Frankensteinish body into life by stressing the innovations of this period in the areas of spirituality, asceticism, the concerns about the body, private life, emotions, and communities that formed around new values, sacred texts, and distinctive types of leadership.

As a new way of looking at old history, late antiquity was successful and rightly so. But it had major blind spots that eventually limited its expansion and elicited push-back. It was too obviously euphemistic and programmatically upbeat. It also had little to say about institutions, political history, economy, and war, which required the return of "the later Roman empire" as a necessary rubric for research in those areas. All this has been much discussed. What concerns us here is what it did to Byzantium. Byzantinists did not willingly surrender one third of their field to make late antiquity possible, nor did they participate much in its creation. As a field, it was rather shoved aside and diminished to its middle and later phases only (641–1204 and 1204–1453 AD, respectively). It was seen as something that came after late antiquity in one small area of its vast terrain, a left-over rump of relatively little interest. Late antiquity inspired little research on middle and late Byzantium.

Moreover, late antiquity drove a wedge between Byzantium and its ancient roots. This had two troubling consequences. The first is that late antiquity appropriated for itself major areas of Byzantine innovation that had world impact, such as the creation of most aspects of post-Constantinian Christianity, including its doctrines, literatures, churches, councils, canons, and institutional structures. Most of this was created in the east by Greek-speaking Christian Romans, i.e., by Byzantines. But scholarship on late antiquity does not situate them within that longer continuum that bridged earlier Roman history and later Byzantium. They appear instead as men of their age, stewing in the same pot with people with whom they could not communicate, such as St. Augustine, who had a completely different cultural and intellectual background and whose future legacies would have radically divergent trajectories. Cyril of Alexandria had little to do with his exact contemporary Augustine. Now, there are many different ways to tell a story, and late antiquity emphasizes synchronicity over diachronicity, which is fair enough. But this robs Byzantium of a culturally productive period in its history and repurposes it in ways that do not promote interest in the left-over rump of its middle and late periods.

Late antiquity was not the first to pull this move. The long-standing tradition in the West of delegitimizing Byzantium, which began already in the Middle Ages, did the same. In their many treatises *Contra errores Graecorum* (*Against the Errors of the Greeks*), some western polemicists argued that the real Roman empire and authentic Christian tradition lasted in the east until about the sixth century, after which the eastern empire became "Greek" and lost its Roman credentials. These theological polemicists chose their cutoff date carefully in order to claim for their side the parts of early Byzantine history that they wanted (the Church Fathers, Councils, Justinian's codification, etc.) and discard the rest, especially what came after. To the Byzantinist, however, what came after appears to have been a natural continuation of precisely these earlier developments. As a result, late antiquity has taken from Byzantium far more than it has given back.

Late antiquity effectively severs Byzantium's connection to its roots in the early Roman period by driving itself as a wedge between the two. In many areas this creates an artificial dead zone that blocks communication between scholars of the ancient world and scholars of Byzantium. For example, late antiquity is not primarily interested in the history of the Greek language and literature, in literary analysis (as it draws mostly from social historians or historians of religion), or in the history of Roman identity. For example, it has never asked what happened to all the self-professed "Greeks" of the second-century empire, or how they became Romans. These issues are not visible within the current paradigm of late antiquity, but are important when it comes to Byzantium, because they are at the heart of its very constitution. Byzantium was not just a rump state that barely survived the Arab conquests of the seventh century: it represented the long-term trajectory and culmination of the Greek, Roman, and Christian cultures of antiquity, both early and "late."

Now that the expansion of late antiquity is slowing down, other paradigms are being proposed that see history in different ways. A purely Byzantinocentric one might be of limited utility and appeal, but are there Big Picture narratives that it can activate or facilitate? One useful rubric for teaching the first millennium is in fact that of "the Roman empire and its heirs," the heirs being primarily the Latin West and the Muslim world; in this scheme, Byzantium is the direct extension of the Roman empire and not its own heir, which would be a bit weird. The Latin West and Islam each picked up, retained, or developed select aspects of the ancient Roman world, mingling them with new cultural elements brought by the Germanic and Arab conquerors of the west and east respectively. This is not far from the approach taken by Chris Wickham in *The Inheritance of Rome: Illuminating the Dark Ages, 400-1000*.[9] Note that by the time that it ends, in 1000 AD, Byzantium was at the peak of its powers compared to its heirs on either side, which had fallen into some disarray, comparatively speaking. This model can be used to teach the first millennium, from Ireland to Iran, and it retains Byzantium in the middle, both geographically and as an axis of continuity.

---

9 C. Wickham, *The Inheritance of Rome: Illuminating the Dark Ages, 400-1000* (London: Viking, 2009).

This rubric can easily be expanded. The Islamic world was not an heir to Rome alone. We must include the Iranian empires that came before it, the Parthian and Sasanian, as Persian culture was fundamentally important to the civilization of the caliphate. A broader schema thus falls into place of two large imperial blocks on either side of Syria, the Graeco-Roman one in the west and the Iranian–Arabic one in the east, which is not to diminish the importance of what was happening between them and along their distant frontiers. This schema accounts for a thousand years and the entire world west of the Indus. It has been proposed by Garth Fowden in his brilliant *Before and After Muhammad: The First Millennium Refocused*.[10] I would not prioritize the history of religions over the history of empires, as Garth seems to do, but I would end this schema, as he does, in the eleventh century, again for imperial reasons: this was when the Seljuks overturned the old order in the Near East and significantly reduced the standing of Byzantium; at the same time, the Christian West began to push back against Muslim states in Spain and Sicily, to attack Byzantium, and to establish colonies in the Near East. Byzantium was no longer the axis of history but a defensive state increasingly squeezed in the middle space.

For the first millennium, at any rate, and even down to 1204, "Byzantium," or Romanía, is for me one of the few identifiable threads that run throughout this story from start to finish, a stubborn survivor who provides a vantage point in the middle of time and space from which both east and west can be surveyed in their long and expansive trajectories.

---

10 G. Fowden, *Before and After Muhammad: The First Millennium Refocused* (Princeton: Princeton University Press, 2014).

Chapter 3

Byzantium for Classicists

When the library of University College London was thinking of cancelling its subscription to *Byzantinische Zeitschrift* on the grounds that it would not be frequently consulted, Arnaldo Momigliano replied that "the problem would not be what to do with *Byzantinische Zeitschrift*, but what to do with a professor of ancient history who remained ignorant of such a periodical."[1]

Peter Brown

Why should classicists care about Byzantium? The problem is not that they should care more about it than they do. It is far worse. The problem is that they already are Byzantinists but don't know it, which makes them bad Byzantinists. They are like scholars working in an archive without knowing why that archive was created, or by whom, or when, or why some documents were included in it and some not. Brilliant scholarship can result even with these limitations, but the latter also create huge blind spots, especially about the overall context of this scholarly activity and its cultural genealogy.

By classicists I mean scholars who study ancient thought and literature and use texts to reconstruct ancient history and society. My focus is primarily on the Greek side of the classical tradition. Byzantium did play a huge role in shap-

---

1 P. Brown, "Arnaldo Dante Momigliano, 1908-1987," *Proceedings of the British Academy* 74 (1988): 405–42 at 423

ing one part of the Latin tradition—Roman law—but apart from that its contribution to Latin studies was small. It did, by contrast, play a much larger role in shaping our knowledge of ancient Roman history. Whereas modern historians of classical Greece rarely have to use Latin texts, historians of any period of Roman history rely heavily on Greek texts, and sometimes primarily on them. This is because the Byzantines, as Romans, were naturally interested in Roman history but had to access all of it through Greek texts. Virtually all Greek texts, whether they were about ancient Rome or not, had to pass through Byzantium in order to reach us. Byzantium was thus more than just a bottleneck in their transmission: it actively determined what made it through and what not, and did so for its own reasons, not to make our study of antiquity easier.

Let us back up and establish a broader context for the argument of this chapter. The ancient world included cultures other than the Greeks and Romans that had their own literary traditions, for example the Egyptians, Assyrians, Phoenicians, and Etruscans. But the only ones that survive in direct transmission are those of the Greeks, Romans, and Jews. They survive—and only partially at that—because later medieval cultures, for their own reasons, saw fit to preserve them. These medieval choices, therefore, determined what survived and what did not. Phoenician and Etruscan literature is, accordingly, entirely lost to us apart from references to it in Greek and Latin texts, or partial translations into those languages. Egyptian texts survive simply because the dry climate of that country preserved ancient papyri and wall paintings, and Assyrian texts were likewise baked in clay tablets. No one *chose* for these texts to survive; they survived for simple material reasons because no one actively destroyed them. In fact, a tiny number of Greek literary texts survive in such forms (inscriptions, tablets, and papyri). Imagine if we had to reconstruct ancient Greek thought from them: that is the daunting task faced by scholars who study the Phoenicians and Etruscans. The reason that classicists are not in that unenviable position is because later, post-classical cultures consciously decided to invest a considerable amount of resources in copying and preserving a specific selection of ancient texts. The Bible, for example, survived in Hebrew, Greek, and Latin, because it was prized by medieval Jews, the Byzantines, and the Catholic world (it also survived in Syriac, Coptic, Arabic, partially in Gothic, and generally in all the languages of groups that accepted Christianity).

It was not at all obvious that ancient Greek literature would survive, and in fact most of it did not survive. Texts could have been (and were) destroyed in fires that consumed whole libraries. These were caused by accidents or by wars, such as when Julius Caesar decided to intervene in Egyptian politics in 48–47 BC and set a major library on fire, or when the Crusaders destroyed Constantinople in 1204 AD. Certain ancient authors such as Kallimachos survived until the early thirteenth century, only to have their lives cut short by Crusader vandalism. It was also a possibility that Christian fundamentalists would take over the eastern empire and systematically rid it of all "pagan" literature. Certainly, powerful voices within the Church did call for Christians to stay away from such corrupting and immoral trash. These voices did not on the whole prevail. But there was no guarantee that a Christian society would provide a safe space for the survival of non-Christian or even anti-Christian literature. In a few cases, texts hostile to Orthodoxy were destroyed, for example the anti-Christian tracts written by Platonists such as Porphyry and Julian, heretical treatises that advocated deviant versions of Christianity, and astrological literature.

But Byzantines did not need to hunt down and actively destroy subversive or immoral literature. All they had to do was simply not invest resources into copying it—i.e., to do nothing at all—and those texts would eventually disappear from circulation. Sheer lack of interest probably explains the loss of most texts that disappeared between the fourth and the twelfth centuries. As in antiquity itself, when texts were also lost through mere indifference and lack of copying, a work did not have to be seen as dangerous or subversive in order to be denied survival. It merely had to be uninteresting or perceived as not useful. What this means is that we have to flip our way of looking at the problem. Instead of asking why some texts were lost or destroyed, we should assume that loss would be the default fate of a text between 300 and 1400: we need then to provide positive reasons for why some texts did survive. We have perhaps 1 percent of ancient Greek literary production, or less. Why did the Byzantines keep that 1 percent?

The field of Classics does not ask this question, even though its research takes place fully within that Byzantine 1 percent (in fact, most classicists focus on a small part of that 1 percent, possibly on 10 percent of the 1 percent). Classicists are not generally trained to know much at all about Byzantium. They take this selection of texts for granted, as if it were a random and perhaps representative sample, or as if the "best" texts were destined to survive. Some regard Byzantium as a culture that is as irrelevant to their field as medieval Japan, and some even dislike it, either because it was Christian or because they have imbibed western prejudices about it (as explained in Chapter 1). According to that view, Byzantium stands for despotism, absolutism, theocracy, blind dogmatism, ignorance, servility, a lack of political culture, fossilized decline, and superstition. What can that have to do with the classical worlds of Greece and Rome? For all of their many faults (including imperialism, slavery, and the seclusion of women), Greece and Rome are still and perhaps rightly perceived as the fonts of many positive social, ethical, political, literary, and philosophical values.

Well, it turns out that the house that classicists live in is a Byzantine house made from a careful Byzantine selection of ancient materials. Whatever they think Byzantium was, classicists need to start revising it quickly, and if they know nothing about it, then they need to start learning. Essentially, they are all just continuing a Byzantine tradition of classical study, and doing so with the materials preserved and the tools invented by the Byzantines themselves. Even more disturbing to them may be the realization that the values and approaches that they bring to the study of classical antiquity may be of Byzantine manufacture. Not to know this is short-sighted in its own right.

I will talk about the importance of Byzantium for Classical Studies in terms of the *selection* of materials; the *tools* of study; *interpretive frameworks*; and its *ongoing utility*.

Selection

Selection is how a canon is created. For example, some texts are valorized as "classical" and so they are preserved, referenced, widely discussed, and have commentaries and scholia written about them. Such choices began to steer the selection process toward a classical canon already in antiquity. I illustrate this in my classics courses through a comparison of Lesbos and Athens, which is also a personal issue for me, as I am both a Lesbian and an Athenian. Athenian authors dominate the classical Greek canon. But next after Athens, Lesbos produced the most potentially canonical poets, thinkers, and authors during the classical period, but we have only fragments of their works, unlike their Athenian counterparts. Athenian hegemony over the Greek world in the fifth century paved the way for the dominance of its literature. This Athenian primacy in the realm of literature was then taken up by the scholars of Alexandria and later by the Romans. Lesbos was marginalized. But imagine if different historical contingencies had resulted in a Lesbian canon rather than an Athenian one. Instead of Aischylos, Sophokles, Plato, and Thucydides, we might all be reading Alkaios, Sappho, Hellanikos, and Theophrastos. Lyric poetry would have survived, not tragedy. What we understand as the Hellenic tradition would have had an utterly different appearance. Even so, by the end of antiquity this general preference for the Athenian tradition over all others had not yet resulted in the complete loss of the alternatives. They were still hanging on.

Roman preferences added another filter of selection and canonization. After their conquest of the Hellenistic world, the Romans made it known that they much preferred the history and literature of classical Greece, i.e., before Alexander, over that of the Hellenistic kingdoms that they had just conquered and liquidated. Their Greek subjects in the first and second centuries AD picked up on these cues, quietly set Hellenistic culture aside, and rediscovered the classical period in a baroque frenzy of neoclassical Atticism that we generally call the Second Sophistic (the role of the Romans here is the subject of a brilliant study by A. J. S. Spawforth, *Greece and the Augustan Cultural Revolution*).[2] The heroes of Marathon were in, while the Ptolemies and Seleucids were out. "Pure" Attic prose was in, the decadence of "Asiatic" rhetoric was out.

So what added filters did Byzantium lay down upon this ongoing process of selection? The emphasis here will be on deliberate choices, to explain the survival of ancient literature in terms of Byzantine priorities. Those priorities operated both continually in the background, for example in decisions about which texts to copy and so pass on to the next generation, especially when resources for literature were scarce, but also during bottlenecks. One bottleneck was the Arab conquests of the seventh century, which boosted the survival rate of the texts which the Byzantines had taken to Constantinople (or which refugees from the conquests brought with them after the 630s). A second bottleneck was the invention of minuscule Greek script in ca. 800, which initiated a long period of textual transcription (known as transliteration): choices had to be made again about which texts to pass on.

Here, then, are the main factors that shaped the Byzantine classical canon (which is our own classical canon). Some of these factors overlapped and so gave a particular text or author greater chances of survival.

One priority inherited from antiquity and intensified in Byzantine times was Atticism in prose, verse, and lexicography. Interest in dialects other than Attic and koine essentially died out in Byzantium and so did most texts written in them. The last text written in another dialect were the Doric hymns of Synesios, the bishop of Kyrene in the early 400s, who

---

2 A. J. S. Spawforth, *Greece and the Augustan Cultural Revolution* (Cambridge: Cambridge University Press 2012).

fancied himself a descendant of Herakles, as we saw. Attic authors such as the tragedians, Plato, Thucydides, Xenophon were prized and thus retained as models of correct diction and also, in some cases, as models of proper prose style. It was possibly this factor which led, in the early Byzantine period, to the replacement of Menander by Aristophanes as the most popular comedian. In antiquity, Menander had been more popular than Aristophanes. Fortunately, that changed in early Byzantine times. These choices had a huge impact on the history of classical scholarship. Byzantine philologists studied primarily these Attic texts and produced their own commentaries and scholia on them. Byzantine dictionaries (such as the tenth-century *Souda*, an encyclopedia of classical studies), along with Byzantine annotated manuscripts of these authors, formed the core of classical scholarship and lexicography when it first appeared in Renaissance Italy: Italian scholars took their cues about the Greek tradition from their contemporary Byzantine teachers.

In terms of history, Byzantine intellectuals were also interested primarily in the Roman, Jewish, and Christian past. They were not particularly interested in the history of the ancient city states. Thucydides and Xenophon survived because of their literary aspects, and Thucydides also because in the early Byzantine period he was a textbook author of speeches and vivid descriptions, and a useful model for historians to imitate (he was imitated by Priskos of Panion, Prokopios of Kaisareia, Agathias of Myrina, and other early Byzantine historians, and he became popular again in the later period, being imitated by the emperor–historian Ioannes VI Kantakouzenos and the Athenian Laonikos Chalkokondyles). The Hellenistic period was of almost no interest to the Byzantines, and so they kept none of its histories or rhetoric, except some works that concerned Rome and Jewish history, the latter represented by Josephos (whose *Jewish War* linked up nicely with prophesies made in the New Testament). Mainly the Byzantines preserved Greek accounts of ancient Roman history (Polybios, Dionysios of Halikarnassos, Appian, Plutarch's *Lives*, Herodian, and many versions of Cassius Dio). This is because the Byzantines were Romans and so naturally interested in their own history. Xiphilinos, who wrote an epitome of Cassius Dio in the 1070s, explicitly noted when he reached the "constitutional settlement" of 27 BC that: "I will now recount each event to the degree that it is necessary, especially from this point on, because our own lives and polity depend fully on what happened at that time. I say this now no longer as Dion of Prousa, who lived under the emperors Severus and Alexander, but as Ioannes Xiphilinos, the nephew of the Ioannes the patriarch, I who am composing this epitome of the many books of Dion under the emperor Michael Doukas."[3]

Homer remained the basis of primary secular education and the touchstone of elite cultivation. To make sense of the myths, the Byzantines kept some ancient mythographic scholarship, for example Apollodoros. The first books of Diodoros of Sicily, which coordinate the prehistories of the major ancient cultures, were also kept and circulated independently of the rest of the work, for they complemented Christian efforts at "universal" chronography that likewise built up a unified table of history from the Creation to the present. Herodotos is an interesting case in this connection. He was neither an Attic author nor a historian of Rome or the Jews. His popularity in Byzantium has to be explained through other factors, including his widely recognized "charm" as an author. Herodotos was indispensable for understanding the historical context of classical literature and, more importantly, for understading the names, references, and allusions that are embedded in it (there are over one thousand proper names in Herodotos). He served as a transition from mythography to the early history not so much of Greece but of the Near East, in which the Byzantines were interested for Scriptural reasons. Indeed, the patriarch Photios in the ninth century read Herodotos not unreasonably as a historian primarily of Persia, who was useful for understanding the con-

---

3 Xiphilinos, *Epitome of Cassius Dio* in *Cassii Dionis Cocceiani historiarum Romanarum quae supersunt*, ed. U. P. Boissevain, 3 vols. (Berlin: Weidmann, 1895–1901), 3:526.

text of the Old Testament. Moreover, Herodotos provided the standard models of ethnography and the names by which the Byzantines classified the barbarians around them, especially the Scythians and the Persians, who recurred as enemies of Byzantium throughout its history.

The Byzantines generally preferred their ancient learning to come in the form of compendia produced right before or during the onset of their own Christian imperial culture. Thus, instead of preserving the ancient sources on which the following works were based—which modern classicists would prefer—we have instead Plutarch's *Moralia*, Athenaios' *Dinner-Sophists*, Aelian's *Various Histories*, Diogenes Laertius' *Lives of the Philosophers*, and Ioannes Stobaios' *Anthology*. In rhetoric too the Byzantines preserved a selection of the original Attic orators and a selection of the Neo-Attic orators of the Roman empire of the second century AD (such as Ailios Aristeides), with nothing surviving from in between. In other words, they wanted original Attic orators and Attic orators who had adapted their craft to a Roman imperial context that most resembled Byzantium. Many textbooks from the ancient tradition of rhetorical theory accompanied this corpus of orations, and the Byzantines added to this tradition with commentaries and textbooks of their own, on both grammar and rhetoric.

The only ancient philosophy in which the Byzantines were interested was Platonism, because it was the most closely related to their theology and provided the most useful conceptual training. This is why they dispensed with everyone else (pre-Socratics, Stoics, Epicureans, Cynics, etc.), whom we have to study through fragments (I am unable to explain the survival of the voluminous Pyrrhonist Sextos Empirikos). The works of Plato were also models of Attic prose, so their survival was twice determined. Therefore, what we have of ancient philosophy are Plato and the Neoplatonists, who wrote closest to the emergence of Christian theology. By this time, Aristotle was regarded (correctly) as a Platonic author, and many of the surviving commentaries on his works were written by Platonic thinkers of the early Byzantine period. We should also not underestimate the popularity of Plato among a few Byzantine thinkers who deviated from the strict path of Christian Orthodoxy and waded into the waters of pagan thought. Judging from certain manuscripts, these Platonic aficionados played a role in the transmission of Plato and the Neoplatonists.

Finally, the Byzantines retained many ancient technical and scientific works because, contrary to the orientalist image of their spirituality and mysticism, theirs were a practical and pragmatic culture. These included medical works, especially the Hippocratic corpus (even the non-Attic parts) and Galen, because Byzantines did not turn only (or even in the first instance) to saints for healing but paid and funded doctors in hospitals. They were also interested in ancient military science and engineering—seeing as the army was the single largest state expense—as well as mathematics and astronomy (among other reasons, for working out problems in the Christian calendar). Ioannes Tzetzes, a classical scholar of the twelfth century, noted that Archimedes, through his written works, continued to benefit mankind.[4] And, in some periods, Byzantine doctors had to pass an examination on Galen in order to be appointed to a paid position.

These were some of the factors that shaped the corpus of Greek literature as we have it today. So when you go into a classics seminar library and stare at rows of the Greek Loebs, Teubners, Oxford Classical Texts, or Budés, know that you are looking at a Byzantine Classical Library. If you are a scholar of classical Greek studies, you are working within a framework established by the Byzantines. It may therefore be necessary, even required, for classicists to know a lot more about this culture. Certainly, a greater level of curiosity is warranted.

The same argument can be made about the sources of our fragments and reports ("testimonia"), not merely about complete texts. For example, many today study the thought

---

4 Ioannes Tzetzes, *Letter* 95 in *Ioannis Tzetzae epistulae*, ed. P. L. M. Leone (Leipzig: Teubner, 1972).

of Herakleitos and Parmenides, but almost no one reads the sixth-century philosopher Simplikios who preserved their words. Simplikios is never cited as the source when the words of Archimedes are repeated, "Give me a place to stand and I will move the earth."[5] These things have been ripped from their Byzantine context and sanitized for use by scholars who no longer know or care where they come from. But that context is important, because this was not a culture of "mere" preservation, a deep freezer from which we can extract pure nuggets of classical learning. It had dynamics of its own, it engaged actively with its own classical sources, and its energies shaped what it preserved for us and what has been lost. For example, few know that Simplikios' philosophical and religious opponent Ioannes Philoponos in Alexandria correctly refuted Aristotle's theory of gravity, a thousand years before Galileo, and seems to have performed experiments to that effect (Galileo knew his work). The fact that this is not broadly known demonstrates that historians of science too are still wedded to the old paradigm that leaps from classical antiquity to early modernity, flying over everything in between.

Tools

Consider also the tools of classical scholarship that the Byzantines gave us. In antiquity, texts were written in vertical columns on horizontally long papyrus rolls, all in capital letters and usually with no spaces between the words. During the early Byzantine period, the codex (book) gradually replaced the papyrus roll, and then, around 800 AD, small case Greek letters were invented. Potentially more text could be fit on each page, though Byzantine scribes often left ample margins for the purposes of annotation. Accent marks began to be used more commonly and spaces placed between words (in addition to abbreviations, which, granted, take some get-

---

5 Simplikios, *On the Physics* 1110.5 in *Simplicii in Aristotelis physicorum libros octo commentaria*, ed. H. Diels, Commentaria in Aristotelem Graeca 9–10, 2 vols. (Berlin: Reimer, 1882–1895).

ting used to). No one wants to go back to ancient technologies in any of these regards, but few classicists know that our format for writing Greek books is essentially Byzantine; modernity added only the printing press to this format, i.e., standardized page numbers and fonts. Byzantine scholars also broke up the ancient commentaries on classical texts, which were previously self-standing volumes of continuous text, and included their most useful glosses in the margins of the texts themselves, thereby annotating them. They also began to produce handy editions that contained a brief biography of a classical author, his works, and commentary material on them in various formats.

The Byzantine scholar was also equipped with various lexica and eventually also with the late tenth-century classical encyclopedia *Souda* that has some thirty thousand entries. These essential aids became the core of classical philology in early modern Europe (the *Souda* was printed as soon as 1499). Dictionaries have genealogies too, and the ones that we use today trace their descent directly back to humanist printings and adaptations of the Byzantine lexica. The latter were, in turn, based on ancient counterparts, but those do not survive. The Byzantine lexica did, moreover, possess a great advantage over their ancient counterparts in that they were fully alphabetized; imagine looking for a word when only the first two letters were alphabetized, or when words are grouped together according to thematic clusters.

Speaking of the alphabet, the names of some of the Greek letters (epsilon, omikron, omega, ypsilon) stem from the Byzantine pronunciation of the language. For example, epsilon—or "short ε"—had to be distinguished from αι, which had come to be pronounced identically. Even though these names are used by modern classicists and philologists—who disastrously try to pronounce the language according to the Erasmian system, which they believe is more authentic— these letter names are inextricably bound to the Byzantine pronunciation. That the ancients had no names for these letters is evident from Plato's *Cratylus* 393d–e. The Byzantines also invented the iota subscript (e.g., switching from ωι to ῳ).

This fact is tacitly acknowledged by some classical series that have abandoned the subscript in favour of a more "authentic" orthography. It goes without saying that they have not also abandoned capital letters and spaces between words.

We should praise here the modern scholars, Nigel Wilson and Eleanor Dickey, who have done the most to illuminate the modes of ancient and Byzantine scholarship (texts, commentaries, lexica, etc.) and the many continuities between the two phases, an area where few dare to tread. Their work has proven that, in the history of classical scholarship, it is illegitimate to leap from antiquity to the Renaissance: a long passage through Byzantium is also necessary, and it is not a detour but a key part of the main story.

Interpretative Framework

Byzantium also laid down fundamental aspects of the general interpretive framework on which Classical Studies still relies. A canon of literature cannot, after all, be studied as classical until after its own proper era has passed and future generations can look back on it as distinct and valorize it as superior. The greater the difference between the valorized classical society of the past and the later one that looks back to it with admiration, the more sharply are drawn the contours of classicism as something "other," as extinct and therefore in need of preservation and study. This perception of difference remained weak for as long as the world was pagan and Greek-speakers in the Roman empire regarded themselves as ethnic Greeks: there were still too many lines of continuity between them and classical antiquity and not enough rupture for an existential difference to be perceived. As Hegel argued, it is tension between successive worldviews—today we might say "identities"—that sparks recognition and generates meaning. To make a culture the object of such reflection requires an external standpoint, and the Christian Romans of Byzantium certainly had one in relation to the Hellenes of antiquity. When they read Homer or gazed upon the statue of a god they understood that they were in the presence of a different culture, whose religion they did not accept and whose national history was not necessarily their own. The Byzantines literally called the ancient pagan world *thyrathen*—that which came from outside the threshold of their own culture. The "inside" of their culture was understood as Christian. The Byzantines were the first to occupy this ambiguous position of difference vis-à-vis their classical culture, and modern western classicists occupy a similar one. Their responses to the underlying challenge have not only been similar to those of the Byzantines: they were actually pioneered by the Byzantines, who were the first classicists in this sense.

Consider the problem of religion. Late pagans could still assume that their gods were the same as the gods of Homer, and so the *Iliad* and *Odyssey* were not for them literary texts from a bygone era but of foundational and even personal relevance to the present. The emperor Julian, for example, certainly thought so (and he believed that Homer's gods—*his* gods—had inspired all canonical ancient authors and were watching over him still). As mentioned above, some Christians wanted nothing to do with Greek mythology and art, and even set about smashing statues to rid their cities of the demons. But these attitudes were marginal when it came to literature and elite education: classical texts were not burned, and even the vandalism and destruction of statues and temples was a haphazard affair. After all, the Christian emperors were first and foremost *Roman* emperors who positively wanted classical statues and themes to adorn their new capital and grace their reigns in general. And some communities simply converted their temples directly into churches without even removing their overt pagan statuary, as happened to the temples on the Akropolis of Athens. The Parthenon became a church dedicated to the Mother of God (the Virgin Mary), but still sported Athena, Poseidon, and Zeus on the pediments.

If they were to continue to enjoy the poems and adorn their cities with the statues of the gods, the Byzantines had to find a work-around to this problem. One of their solutions, which is fundamentally constitutive of all subsequent classical studies, was to treat the texts as mere literature and the statues as mere art. We might even make a rather grandiose claim here: it was only when these texts and statues were stripped of their religious meaning that the categories of "literature" and "art" fully came into being. The Church Father Gregorios of Nazianzos, who had studied in Athens at the same time as Julian, made a case for Greek literature along these lines in his response to Julian. His attacks on his former classmate were intemperate and are embarrassing today, but he makes the claim that the classical texts, which he loved, were not inherently religious and could be studied by anyone who had the right education, regardless of religion.[6] Gregorios' friend Basileios of Kaisareia (that is, Basil of Caesarea), a Church Father who had studied in Athens at the same time too, wrote a brief treatise on the subject: *To Young Men on How They Might Benefit from Greek Literature* (where "Greek" also means "pagan").[7] The cherry-picking but broadly tolerant approach that he recommends ("keep the good stuff and discard the bad stuff, such as the gods and the immorality") was subsequently followed by most educated Byzantines. Basileios' treatise was popular in early modern Europe and, coming from one of the most important Fathers in the Christian tradition, authorized the labours of many humanists.

That we can read Homer today as just literature without worrying about the religious implications of the gods proves how successful this approach was: it is embedded so deeply in our reactions to the text that we don't usually even notice it. (By way of comparison, we still cannot do the same with the New Testament, at least not without pushback or defensive disclaimers.)

Likewise for art. As some Christian zealots were going around smashing and defacing statues, the Christian emperors passed legislation creating a space for the statues to

---

6 Gregorios of Nazianzos, *Oration* 4: *Invective against Julian.*

7 Basil of Caesarea, *To Young Men on How They Might Benefit from Greek Literature* (full reference in the Further Reading for Chapter 3).

survive by reclassifying them explicitly as "art," as opposed to the value of their former "divinity," which they rejected (*Theodosian Code* 16.10.8, 15, 18). The emperors sent agents around the eastern Mediterranean to gather up the best statues and artworks and used them to adorn Constantinople–New Rome. In the century after its foundation, Constantinople became the greatest repository of classical art in all of history, second only to Rome. The public spaces of the hippodrome, the fora, the baths, the colonnaded streets, and special collections were populated by hundreds of statues, including many ancient masterpieces. The court official (and eunuch) Lausos created a collection that included Olympian Zeus (by Pheidias), the Aphrodite of Knidos (by Praxiteles), the Hera of Samos, the Athena of Lindos, and others. The Byzantines were thus the first people in history to collect and admire ancient statuary who did not believe in the existence of the divinities themselves.

For Byzantine classical scholars, this created fascinating opportunities for the interplay of text and image. For example, when they read about the gods in ancient literature, or even about specific statues of the gods, they did not need to imagine them for they had in their city a selection of authentic images themselves. Sometimes they ventured specific identifications between statues that they read about and those that could see in, say, the forum of Constantine. And when they praised a contemporary woman for having, say, a nose like that of Aphrodite, they all had a vivid, shared, and authentic mental image of what that was.

Unfortunately all the ancient art gathered in Constantinople was destroyed in the fires and wars that periodically ravaged the capital (excepting a part of the Serpent Column from Delphi and an Egyptian obelisk, that are both standing in the hippodrome). This resulted in a curious paradox in the survival of ancient literature and art, a topic on which Jaś Elsner and I gave a joint presentation in 2014 at the Getty museum in Los Angeles. I noted that when it comes to Greek literature, we have pretty much what the Byzantines kept, the best stuff that they selected for themselves, whereas Jaś

noted that when it comes to art we tend to have the sec-
ond-rate stuff and Roman-period copies that they left behind
in the provinces and didn't bother to take to Constantinople.

Ongoing Utility

In sum, Byzantine choices and Byzantine history played a
fundamental role in shaping the classical canon as we have it
and many of the modes through which we interact with it. Classicists are basically Byzantinists, whether they know it (or like
it) or not. Moreover, Byzantine material continues to yield trea-
sures that advance classical scholarship. I want to close with
two striking illustrations of the ongoing utility of Byzantine
sources. Philologists (especially editors of the ancient texts)
will of course always need to consult Byzantine manuscripts,
but I am here interested more in the work of ancient historians. At any moment, their research may take them around a
corner and straight into a Byzantine text.

One of the mysteries in Herodotos' account of the battle
of Marathon is how the Athenian phalanx managed to charge
the Persian army when it had, for many days, been avoiding
battle in the plain out of fear of the Persian cavalry. Where
did the cavalry go? Consider the entry in the *Souda* (X 444)
on the phrase "the horsemen are away." It says that Miltia-
des ordered the charge when Ionians in the Persian army sig-
nalled to him that Datis was departing and the cavalry were
not present to engage.

Historians of the invention of coinage cannot but turn
to the testimony of the *Etymologicum magnum* (a lexicon of
the twelfth century), under the word *obeliskos*, according to
which money was first minted by one Pheidon of Argos. He
then used the coins to buy spits, which he dedicated to Hera.
Lo and behold, the excavators of the Argive Heraion, the
ancient temple in Argos, found a bundle of archaic iron spits
dedicated to the goddess.

Byzantine testimony is sometimes dismissed or at least
qualified as "late." But its mere chronology is not a reflection of
its value. In the conservative context of classical study, infor-

mation could be transmitted from one lexicon or scholar to the next over the centuries and not change much in between. Byzantine scholarship was thus a direct extension (and refinement) of ancient scholarship, and its roots sometimes ran deep into the irrecoverable past, such as to the invention of coinage at the end of the Greek Dark Age. Consider a more striking example. In the sixth century, the Constantinopolitan scholar Stephanos prepared a dictionary of place-names and their corresponding ethnic names (the *Ethnika*). The entry for "Samylia" notes that it was a city in Karia built by Motylos, who hosted Paris and Helen, presumably right before the Trojan War. Nothing else is known about Motylos, except that his name is likely a version of the Hittite king Muwatalli, who ruled in Asia Minor during the Bronze Age. It is anyone's guess how this information was transmitted in classical antiquity (which almost completely ignored the Hittites' existence) in order to reach Stephanos.

Therefore, for the purposes of training classical scholars, cut-off points between antiquity and Byzantium are not helpful and are a recent invention. In the nineteenth century, before the invention of the field of Byzantine Studies and before classicists began to professionally disdain Christian material, the greatest classical scholars were equally adept in working with ancient, early Christian, and Byzantine texts, and did not essentialize them into separate fields with boundaries policed by disciplinary labels. Think of Theodor Mommsen, Eduard Schwartz, and John Bagnell Bury, as well as, in the twentieth century, Arnaldo Momigliano and A. H. M. Jones, and now Eleanor Dickey. In 1975, Momigliano proposed that "anything Greek we meet in our past is inextricably combined with Rome and with Christianity" (whose combination, of course, is just Byzantium). Therefore, "classicism [...] is by definition a confrontation with Rome and Christianity even before it involves the Greeks." To this challenge Hugh Lloyd-Jones, Regius Professor of Greek at Oxford, responded, with considerable sarcasm, that he did "my best to prevent my reading from being colored by my knowledge of anything that happened later." The problem, of course, is that his "reading" was shaped by what "happened later," whether he knew and liked it or not.[8] Wilful ignorance ill-befits a scholar.

I invite classical Hellenists to think about what their field is actually doing. If they are committed to the superlative and inherent value of the classical authors, and believe that it is imperative that we continue to interpret Homer, Plato, and Euripides, or, say, the workings of Athenian democracy, then Byzantium probably has little to offer to this labour of interpretation. I know of no Byzantine analysis of the tragedians, Homer, or Athenian democracy, that can compete with, or claim a place beside, the best modern readings. Even so, Byzantium should be recognized as actively preserving these texts for positive reasons of its own and not by way of "cold storage." It should no longer be essentialized as an alien Orthodox culture whose concerns were radically different from those of modern classicists. It too engaged with the classics, in some familiar and some different ways (for example, we cannot possibly hope to match Byzantine efforts at Attic prose composition). This kind of classical scholarship—which studies the deep thoughts of the ancient thinkers or the enduring values of their societies—is probably the most honest approach for a field that names itself Classical and stakes a claim that its materials are uniquely important, whether philosophically or in terms of their foundational importance or relevance.

But this is not what most classicists are doing these days. They are treating the cultures of Greece and Rome as more or less equivalent to any other in history, to be studied through the application of the same analytical categories, coupled with specialized linguistic skills, in order to explore every nook and cranny for the sake of increasing our knowledge and understanding of the whole of history. If this is the case, however, what purpose does the divide between classics and Byzantium serve? Both depend on the same linguistic train-

---

8 Hugh Lloyd-Jones, reply by Arnaldo Momigliano, "Bearing Gifts," *New York Review of Books*, January 22, 1976. I thank Jake Ransohoff for this reference.

ing. Why then are so many students trained in ancient Greek only to produce countless unread dissertations on Homer, when we lack any monographs on the classical scholarship of the *Souda*, Ioannes Tzetzes, Theodoros Prodomos, or Eustathios of Thessalonike, the greatest Homeric commentator of all time?

The answer is that classics programs will generally not hire scholars who work on this material, on the assumption that they are not really classicists. Let us rephrase this in order to see clearly how weird it is: professional classicists apparently believe that scholars who have learned Homeric and Attic Greek well enough to read the likes of Eustathios of Thessalonike; who can toggle between the classical text and a later commentary on it (also written in Greek); who can meaningfully discuss the ongoing relevance and importance of a classical text in a post-classical Christian society; who are working on understudied material and so producing original and ground-breaking work on texts that were central to the evolution of the classical tradition from antiquity to the present ... that these scholars are not *really* classicists. Something has gone horribly wrong here, and the problem must lie on a deep ideological level.

Chapter 4

Byzantium Was Not Medieval

It seems, O Italians, that you no longer remember our ancient harmony. [...] But no other nations were ever as harmonious as the Greeks and the Italians. And this was only to be expected, for science and learning came to the Italians from the Greeks. And after that point, so that they need not use their ethnic names, a New Rome was built to complement the Elder one, so that all could be called Romans after the common name of such great cities, and have the same faith [Christianity]. And just as they received that most noble name from Christ, so too did they take upon themselves the national name [Roman]. And everything else was common to them: magistracies, laws, literature, city councils, law courts, piety itself; so everything was common to the people of Elder Rome and New Rome. But O how things have changed!

Georgios Akropolites,
Byzantine diplomat and historian
(thirteenth century)[1]

"Medieval" has both a specific and a generic sense. The specific sense refers to the history of western Europe between the fall of Rome and the Renaissance or early modernity. Its geography is broadly coterminous with the use of Latin as a

---

I Georgios Akropolites, *Against the Latins* 2.27 in *Georgii Acropolitae opera*, ed. A. Heisenberg, rev. P. Wirth, 2 vols. (Stuttgart: Teubner, 1978), 2:64, my translation.

learned language and with the jurisdiction of the Church of Rome. The huge majority of practising "medievalists" study England, France, northern Italy, and to a slightly lesser extent the German lands, and there is now a significant interest in Scandinavia. Slavic cultures and Byzantium are considered separate fields. Southern Spain and southern Italy fall into an almost different field, or quasi-field, the "medieval Mediterranean," entry into which virtually requires that one work on "contacts" across religious communities. This specific sense of the medieval world accounts for the vast majority of papers given at medieval conferences, the articles published in medieval journals, and the areas of expertise of those hired as medievalists. These areas include English peasants, French queens, and German nuns, but rarely Slavic chiefs, Byzantine tax systems, or Islamic thought.

If language is a unifying thread of this field, it is Latin. Medievalists are not normally trained in Slavonic, Greek, or Arabic. If religion is another thread, it is the Catholic Church. In this field, "medieval Christianity" is understood to be that of western and central Europe, even though the majority of Christians during the medieval period lived in the east, in the Slavic, Byzantine, and Muslim-ruled lands, and farther east than that too. Medievalists (again, in the specific sense) may have an idea of what made Orthodoxy different from Catholicism, but they will normally not know the difference among Melkites, Jacobites, and Nestorians, even though the last Church (the Church of the East) included millions of followers in lands stretching as far as India and China.

By contrast, the generic sense of medieval broadly includes the history of all regions of the world after the fall of its ancient "classical" empires (roughly between the fifth and the seventh centuries AD) and before the onset of the early modern gunpowder empires and other distinctively modern developments in the fifteenth century. It is thus possible to refer to medieval India and medieval Japan. "Medieval" in this generic sense refers to chronology and little else. Medievalists in the specific sense, who are mostly western academics and therefore strive in theory to be inclusive, sometimes try to open their specific (western) field to all those that are encompassed by the generic sense of the term. Their journals will strive to attract submissions on non-western cultures; medieval lecture series at universities will consider inviting speakers on non-western topics; book series (such as the present one) will ambitiously expand their scope outside western Europe; and debates will be held on whether there is any sense in studying world history under the medieval rubric, or whether it really fits only French queens and German nuns, if it even fits them to begin with.

I say this because the term medieval—referring to a "middle" or "in-between" period—is inherently problematic. As a periodization it was invented by scholars during the early Renaissance to refer to what they perceived as a crummy phase in the history of their societies between the fall of Rome and their own rediscovery of the virtues of classical antiquity, such as proper Ciceronian Latinity. But this may not be the best way to periodize history. For one thing, no one in the medieval world would have understood what that meant: their lives were not "in-between," and the priorities of the early humanists need not bind us forever. Some historians have accordingly sought other reasons to preserve the category (for example, in economic or religious history), or they have proposed broader or more contracted schemas. Jacques Le Goff, for example, has advocated a long Middle Ages, starting in late Rome and ending in the eighteenth century, when, he believes, the European nation-states properly emerged.[2] But the opposite trend can also be observed. The field of "late antiquity" has been pushed by some to the early Carolingians (i.e., to the ninth century), whereas at the other end some historians of early modernity have reached back to claim everything after the twelfth century, when the European economy embarked upon a trajectory that would arc to modernity. With late antique and early modern historians

2 J. Le Goff, *Faut-il vraiment découper l'histoire en tranches?* (Paris: Seuil, 2014).

claiming so much territory, that leaves only a rump Middle Ages squeezed around the turn of the millennium.

Byzantium has little standing or stake in this debate. It never experienced any loss of contact with its ancient literary patrimony, or rupture in its political or social continuity, such that it had to rediscover the past later through a process of cultural reawakening. There could be no Byzantine Renaissance because nothing had died that needed to be revived; some eras were more flourishing than others but there were no ruptures that led to the creation of new identities (at least not before the onset of western colonialism after 1204). There is another way in which Byzantium is different from many western medieval societies. The medieval world is a fuzzy construct in both time and space and it is never clear whether a particular society belongs to it properly. But Byzantium, the primary referent in the field of Byzantine Studies is by contrast extremely easy to identify. There is no ambiguity or chronological fuzziness here: the field is defined by the history of a particular state, which one can always spot in the evidence, and that state harboured a Greek-speaking Roman and Orthodox society that had a distinctive national culture. Byzantium does not need the label "medieval" in order to stand forth with clarity and definition in the historical record.

Now, one can argue for a "long Byzantium" by extending it earlier into Roman history, to the second and even the first century AD, as I proposed in Chapter 2. And one can also study the dissemination of Byzantine culture abroad, especially to the Slavic world, for instance under the rubric of "the Byzantine Commonwealth."[3] But these extensions of the field pose no identity-crises comparable to those that Medieval Studies confronts. Byzantium even had a proper name that was widely used by its people from the fourth century to the fifteenth: Romanía. It was a specific entity. It was not part of the Catholic world and had almost no Latin after 600 AD. It did not take to crusading (to put it mildly). Its social structure

---

3 D. Obolensky, *The Byzantine Commonwealth: Eastern Europe, 500–1453* (London: Weidenfeld and Nicolson, 1971).

and law were effectively those of the later Roman empire, and did not match anything in western Europe. Its monks did not have orders and were mostly not ordained. There are no analytical gains to be had for calling this society "medieval."

The Byzantines themselves definitely regarded the western medieval world as different and foreign, increasingly so over time. At first, it appeared as a hodge-podge collection of barbarian tribes and principalities, among which those of the Franks stood out as more important. But contacts with it were not especially dense before the eleventh century, as Byzantium was preoccupied with the Persians and Arabs in the east and the Avars and Bulgars in the Balkans. With the rise of the Reform papacy and the coming of the Normans to southern Italy, relations became thicker and much more tense. The religious rift between the western Latin Church and the eastern Greek one, which existed since the fourth century, widened over time, and the Fourth Crusade exposed the hostile intentions toward Byzantium of a wide coalition of prominent western powers. By this point, the Byzantines were calling the westerners collectively "Franks," "Latins," or "Italians," and developed various images and stereotypes by which to reify and represent them as a group. The same took place on the other side, as we saw in Chapter 1. Between the thirteenth and the seventeenth century, the West conquered, colonized, and ruled parts of the Byzantine world, subjecting its people to regimes of domination that were marked by perceptions of ethnic and religious difference. To be sure, there was some exchange, collaboration, and hybridity, but we should not privilege these simply because they are methodologically and morally appealing: by and large, differences hardened over time.

For all their commonalities, exchanges, and points of contact, the Latins and the Byzantines belonged effectively to different civilizations, which makes it hard and even counter-productive to lump them together under a single rubric, whether "medieval" or something else. I will explain a few of those differences. As a state, Romanía was a continuation of the ancient Roman polity, and a single law held sway over most of its dominions and subjects. Some may have enjoyed fiscal perks due to office or court title, but Roman society was otherwise regimented by a relatively homogenous legal grid. There were no fixed classes, hereditary titles of nobility, or castes, and so anyone could, in both theory and practice, rise from a humble origin to occupy positions of power, even the imperial throne itself. Society was not governed or dominated by a hereditary nobility, nor was there a local aristocracy that held formal rights over specific territories. Instead, it was governed by magistrates appointed by the court or the centralized bureaucracy to hold office in turn for limited periods. The monarchy was never in principle hereditary, and was defined in relation to the polity of the Roman people, as its executive power and benefactor. These Romans had a strong conception of being "free citizens," and regularly deposed emperors who appeared to have failed in their duties.

Romanía was also a "state" in a strong sense. It retained from antiquity a sophisticated tax structure that generated substantial revenues, which it used to maintain standing state armies and the most impressive capital city in the entire Christian world. The tax demands of the state stimulated production and thereby boosted the local economies, making Byzantium wealthier than its western counterparts. This was the reason why western visitors were regularly astonished by the amount of coin that the Byzantine emperor had at his disposal: it was not all a show. To deploy this state apparatus, the emperor simply gave orders to his magistrates; he did not need to engage in internal diplomacy, haggling over rents and services with recalcitrant nobles who were entrenched in their local power-bases or commanded effectively private armies. They had small retinues, but at no point in Roman history before 1204 did private aristocratic armies challenge the centralized state or dare to defy it. Byzantium in the tenth century resembled the Roman empire of the fourth century more than it resembled any contemporary western medieval state.

Moreover, the Byzantines did not recognize the pope as the supreme leader of the Christian world, even before they began to suspect that the Catholic Church was a hotbed of heresy and un-Christian practices. Not knowing Latin, they were generally unaware, uninterested, and uninvolved in intellectual developments that were taking place in the West (they tried to catch up in the fourteenth century, but it was too late). This means that intellectual historians of the medieval West and of Byzantium do not *have* to study each other's materials, and so they generally don't. But it also means that the Byzantines had little say in the intellectual trajectories taken by the West on a range of issues, for example the key idea of Romanness. The Byzantine version was closely linked to its authentic Roman roots—that is, to a Roman nation having its own sovereign *res publica* (*politeia* in Greek)—but in the West all kinds of novel ideas were proposed about this, for example making the pope the arbiter of the Roman tradition (an idea that would have baffled a Roman of the Christian empire of late antiquity) or calling the German kings "emperors of the Romans" (an idea that apparently baffled everyone at the time, as no one could explain who these Romans were of whom he was the emperor). The entire western tradition of political thought and legal theory was based on these new fictions and completely disregarded the existence of a Roman *populus* and Roman *res publica* in the east, dismissing them inaccurately but conveniently as "Greek." The Latin West eventually developed a rough notion of its own identity as an agglomerated Catholic civilization—the core of the later idea of "Europe"—and this notion did not include Byzantium. It is still not clear whether it does today.

I am not optimistic about efforts to include it now, largely because of the asymmetrical relationship that exists between the two fields and their different states of development and representation in academic research.

There are far more medievalists than there are Byzantinists, and their field is much bigger. Compare, in terms of attendance, book exhibits, and the publications that emerge from them, the annual International Congress on Medieval Studies at Kalamazoo (over five hundred and fifty *sessions* of papers and other events) or its now bigger equivalent at Leeds to the Byzantine Studies Conference in the US (about sixty to seventy papers delivered), the Spring Symposium of Byzantine

Studies in the UK, or the International Congress of Byzantine Studies (which is held only every five years). Medieval Studies is also far more advanced theoretically and in terms of experimental, cutting-edge scholarship. Byzantine Studies is still struggling to break free from nineteenth-century paradigms (e.g., about race), is still largely in denial over the Roman question, and is a more conservative and repetitive field. Moreover, Medieval Studies has had far more resources placed at its disposal by the wealthiest countries on the planet, where the most advanced research centres are located because those countries have a national stake in the history of "their" corner of the medieval world. In some respects, the field of Medieval Studies is an agglomeration of relatively siloed national histories that are united by a small group of scholars who write "umbrella" scholarship on the medieval world broadly. Byzantine Studies does not enjoy comparable advantages; in fact, some of the nations with a stake in Byzantine history have a tense relationship with it, as their goal is to *extract* their national history from the Byzantine (Roman) context, not necessarily to demonstrate their continuity with or from it.

These asymmetries result in an imbalance of interpretive labour imposed on members of the two fields with respect to each other. Byzantinists generally have to know a fair amount about the medieval West, if not necessarily to keep up with its latest developments; it is one of the fields on which they are regularly tested in graduate school; and they will often be trained in Latin in addition to Greek and other languages necessary for their research. Medievalists need to know nothing whatsoever about Byzantium apart from the fact that it existed, and very few of them can read Greek. I have met distinguished scholars of medieval monasticism who do not know, and were quite perplexed to learn, that Byzantine monks were generally not ordained, did not belong to "orders," and that the Byzantine Church did not undergo overhauls of Reform as in the West. This implies that on a fairly fundamental level, the field of Medieval Studies does not require its experts to read even a single book on the Byzantine side of the questions that interest them, even though that is where Christian monasticism began, first flourished, and laid down its fundamental modes and orders. In exchanges between the two fields, it is thus the Byzantinist who has to provide the common platform, make Byzantium accessible, and do the work of imagining what Byzantium looks like to a medieval scholar—not the reverse.

I can think of few historians who are proficient in both fields and build overarching theses that bring them together (they include Mike McCormick, Chris Wickham, Nikos Chrissis, and Teresa Shawcross). Otherwise, the flow of ideas and models has generally gone from Medieval to Byzantine Studies, for example in the study of agricultural life, the family, and gender. I cannot think of a historical model, methodology, concept, or general influence that has travelled in the opposite direction.

Before going further, I should note a big exception to this asymmetry: art history. I am not an art historian and so am reluctant to represent this field, but I do try to keep up with it and believe that something different is going on there. The general impression that I have is that Byzantine art historians see themselves as art historians first who only happen to work on Byzantium, rather than primarily as Byzantinists (which is what I am). The field of art history is configured in such a way that it not only facilitates but requires art historians who work on different cultures to talk to each other as much or more than they talk to historians or philologists who specialize in their specific periods of focus. Their concerns, interpretive models, and terms of art are different from those of general historians and philologists. In the case of Byzantine art history, they are dealing moreover with a body of artifacts—chiefly icons, ivories, reliquaries, and manuscript images—that were highly portable and did travel from Byzantium to the West, where they exerted influence, though the reverse seems to have happened to a much lesser degree, certainly before the thirteenth century. Byzantine art has also established a certain cachet and prestige in the contemporary art scene in the West, including museums. So art is an area where (a) Byzantium gave models to the medieval West and (b) medieval and Byzantine art historians have established better channels of balanced communication and discussion than have the other disciplines.

I do not believe, however, that this model can easily be replicated elsewhere. For one thing, I suspect that the training of medieval art historians does include some exposure to Byzantine materials to a far greater extent than happens in the other disciplines (where it might typically be zero). And art history is as much a set of methodologies for analyzing a distinct class of artifacts, methodologies which vary less across neighbouring cultures than might happen when working, for example, on linguistically-bound literatures or social formations.

Can Byzantine Studies as a whole be integrated into a medieval Big Tent? I do not think this would work, in part because the field of Medieval Studies is not really open to such a merger, despite its professed but occasional commitment to inclusivity. If its scholars never bother to read the latest on Byzantium, they are not going to require their graduate students to do so either. Exclusive, even dismissive, attitudes are still prevalent, if rarely spoken. At a panel discussion of this question, one medievalist flatly declared, "I do not want to belong to a field that includes Byzantium and the Slavs." This was refreshingly candid. The unctuous piety of "inclusivity" stifles only the expression of such attitudes, not their existence, and this creates a gap between our rhetoric and the reality of our fields. It is risky to build on hollow expectations, especially for junior scholars whose careers depend in myriad ways on the approval of the old guard. Forget the "global Middle Ages": here is it difficult to secure the inclusion of even the Slavic world, for all that it has been amply demonstrated that its exclusion makes nonsense of European history in both medieval and modern times.[4]

In 2015 I attended a roundtable discussion of the theme "Byzantium and the Middle Ages: Bosom Buddies or Uneasy

---

4 C. Raffensperger, *Reimagining Europe: Kievan Rus' in the Medieval World* (Cambridge, MA: Harvard University Press, 2012); J. Darwin, *After Tamerlane: The Rise and Fall of Global Empires, 1400–2000* (New York: Bloomsbury, 2008), 120.

Allies?", at the International Congress on Medieval Studies at Kalamazoo. The audience was engaged in the discussion and broadly supportive of Byzantinist positions. But my colleague Pasha Johnson (curator of the Hilandar Research Library at Ohio State University) astutely thought to ask how many audience members identified as Byzantinists. Almost all raised their hands. This deflating group experience vividly illustrated who is and who is not engaged in the conversation. The medievalists had simply not shown up.

Theoretical efforts made by individual historians to fit Byzantium into a medieval template have so far relied on bad ideas or contain a covert politics that should be resisted. Among the bad ideas is the concept of feudalism. In the early-to mid-twentieth century, some historians attempted to force Byzantium into the Marxist schema of a progression from slave society (the ancient Roman empire) to feudalism. This alleged transition took place in the West immediately upon the fall of the Roman empire, but Byzantium could not just be left out of this totalizing narrative. When did it become feudal? Some historians asserted that this happened (belatedly) in the eleventh century, or else in the twelfth under the Komnenian dynasty, or, if not before that, then certainly in the fourteenth century under the Palaiologan dynasty. Let us say that the rubric of feudalism did not catch on among most Byzantinists as it did not explain anything that could not be explained better in Byzantine terms; it imported a wide range of irrelevant associations and implications from the medieval West that had no place in Byzantium; and, finally, the concept of feudalism came under severe criticism among western medievalists themselves toward the end of the twentieth century, making it an even worse investment for Byzantinists, who were largely giving up on overtly Marxist models at roughly the time that the Soviet Union collapsed.

Évelyn Patlagean's 2007 book *Un Moyen Âge grec: Byzance XIe–XVe siècle*[5] was thus an odd outlier. Patlagean was

---

5 É. Patlagean, *Un Moyen Âge grec: Byzance XIe–XVe siècle* (Paris: Albin Michel, 2007).

among those Byzantinists most attuned to developments in medieval historiography, and rare in her deep grounding in the *Annales* school of interpretation. However, the concept by which she justified including Byzantium in the medieval world, even to the point of giving it its own "Middle Ages," was that of feudalism, though it is not a version of feudalism that I recognize from medieval scholarship (it originated, she argues, in the ancient Roman empire). More than ten years have passed since publication, and it does not seem that this idea is catching on. And one should note again, even in the title of the book, that the price that Byzantium has to pay for admission into the medieval club is the surrender of its Roman claims and the adoption of a "Greek" face, which conforms to western biases.

In my view there was nothing feudal about Byzantium in the eleventh and twelfth centuries, except that the emperors did occasionally use western forms to bind their Latin followers as "vassals." In the thirteenth century, it did experience versions of various feudal orders but largely because they were directly imported by the western colonizers of its dismembered empire in the aftermath of the Fourth Crusade. And if the term feudal is used for domestic Byzantine relationships in the fourteenth and fifteenth centuries, it should be taken in a loose sense (in contrast to the empire's dealings with western powers and individuals, which were conducted often in the forms and language of western vassalage).

Byzantinists should also be wary of the politics that sometimes lurk behind western European gestures of magnanimous inclusion. Specifically, Byzantium is sometimes caught up in debates in Europe over the inclusion or exclusion of Islam. In 2008, Sylvain Gouguenheim published his controversial *Aristote au Mont-Saint-Michel*.[6] A goal of the book was to push back against the idea that Europe needed any infusions of Arabic thought in order to make intellectual progress, specifically of philosophy based on the Arab reception

---

6 S. Gouguenheim, *Aristote au Mont-Saint-Michel: Les racines grecques de l'Europe chrétienne* (Paris: Seuil, 2008).

of the Greek classics. Europe or the West did not need such help, Gouguenheim maintained, because the original texts of ancient philosophy were possessed by the Byzantines, who transmitted them to Latin scholars. To make this argument, Byzantium is cast as an integral part of the western or Christian world whose trajectory eventually led to modern Europe. But Byzantinists should be cautious in accepting this potentially poisoned embrace. The argument makes a tactical and even instrumental use of Byzantium in order to exclude Arabic thought from the intellectual DNA of the West. As far as I could tell, doing justice to Byzantium on its own terms is not part of the agenda. Coming after centuries of western abuse of Byzantium as a decadent, degraded, and entirely unclassical and non-western culture, this rather cynical invocation of it by Europe's cultural conservatives should at least have been accompanied by a full reckoning of how and why they got it wrong all this time and how they intend to rectify past injustices, even as they are embarking upon new ones.

While we are on the subject of thorny political issues, we might as well go all in and raise the matter of the Crusades. It has not escaped the notice of Byzantinists that a decades-long movement has taken place among some medievalists to rehabilitate the Crusades as acts of deeply sincere piety that were not motivated by worldly concerns, even as acts of Christian "love."[7] It should come as no surprise that many Byzantinists will remain unpersuaded by this thesis, and not only because it sought from the beginning to dethrone the classic history of the Crusades by Steven Runciman, one of our own tribe, as it were, even if many ways an unconventional affiliate. Runciman viewed many of the Crusades' protagonists with sympathy, but he thought that the movement as a whole was destructive and did not redound to the honour

---

7 J. Riley-Smith, "Crusading as an Act of Love," *History* 65 (1980): 177–92, followed up by Riley-Smith, *The First Crusade and the Idea of Crusading* (Philadelphia: University of Pennsylvania Press, 1986), an approach which can be said to have started an entire school of Crusade Studies.

of the faith. It was this picture that a number of prominent medievalists sought to change, and in doing so they verged close to—or actually entered upon—what can only be called an apologia for violent aspects of medieval Catholicism. Faith-driven scholarship, as much of this patently is, creates uncomfortable spaces where others are reluctant to enter for fear of giving offence, and so the pushback from other medievalists against this overtly pietistic and upbeat reading of the Crusades has taken longer than it otherwise might have. Recent publications suggest that is well under way.

Byzantium, of course, was the eventual victim of a Crusade, which inflicted more destruction upon this Christian society than any Christian power had yet delivered to another up to that point in history. What complicates this event for our discussion is that this was not a routine war between conventional rivals, albeit an extremely destructive one. It was in fact an act of aggression by one civilization against another, in the sense that both the aggressor and the victim were acutely aware of their ethnic, religious, political, and cultural differences, and the extreme violence that accompanied the destruction of Constantinople was driven by the self-awareness on the part of many crusaders of those differences. Those "heretical Greeks" had it coming for "siding with the Saracens" and "rebelling against the Holy Father" (i.e., not submitting to Rome).

It does not help, therefore, that the standard history of the Fourth Crusade (by D. E. Queller and T. Madden) reads like an apologia for the Catholic armies.[8] Each step in the crusaders' thinking, as they were borne along toward the fateful *dénouement* of April 13, 1204, is weighed carefully, justified, and presented with sympathy for their underlying values and anguished moral choices. Yet their Byzantine victims are not given comparable consideration. The ample Byzantine testimony about the event, containing a horrified and bitter reaction, is barely utilized and, when it is, it is dismissed as politi-

---

8 D. E. Queller and T. Madden, *The Fourth Crusade: The Conquest of Constantinople*, 2nd ed. (Philadelphia: University of Pennsylvania Press, 1997).

cally biased. The narrative implies that, in their dysfunctional state, the "Greeks" were used to this kind of thing and even welcomed their new western overlords, preferring them over their own rulers. The authors carefully tally the western loot but not the Byzantine victims.

When I heard Tom Madden give a talk on the Fourth Crusade in 2005, I felt like I was hearing Donald Rumsfeld, the Secretary of Defense, talk about the US invasion of Iraq in 2003 ("welcomed by the liberators," "we don't do body counts," "good intentions gone wrong," and the like). Madden denied that the destruction of Constantinople exacerbated the widening rift between the two Churches, which is contradicted by Byzantine testimony produced soon after the sack of the city and for many centuries thereafter. When asked directly about it, he said that he disagreed with pope John Paul II's public apology in Greece for the crimes committed against Constantinople by "Latin Christians." If you think I am distorting Tom Madden's views, consider that soon afterward (in 2008) he published a book that celebrated the similarities between the United States and Rome as imperial powers, because they both brought security and prosperity to the lands they conquered. Madden there defends the invasion of Iraq and the doctrine of preemptive attack, and compares George W. Bush to Cincinnatus. Rome and the US did not seek to control others through conquest but rather to teach them how to use power responsibly.[9]

So, yes, we clearly have some major issues to work through. Medievalist colleagues assure me that these are not typical or representative views, but they are the views of a leading historian of the Crusades, and of the Fourth Crusade in particular. It also does not appear that the average medievalist knows more about the Byzantine side of the story than Madden does.

Right before they seized Constantinople in mid-April 1204, the leaders of the Crusade had deliberated and agreed

9 T. Madden, *Empires of Trust: How Rome Built—and America Is Building—A New World* (New York: Dutton, 2008).

on how to divide the prospective spoils among themselves. They intended to dismember the Byzantine empire and install their own governing classes over its former territories. This did not work out entirely according to plan, for the Byzantines regrouped more effectively than was anticipated. But the Latins still remained a powerful presence in Greece and the Aegean for centuries, ruling over scattered dukedoms, principalities, outposts, and trading zones. In Greece today this is called the period of the *Frangokratia*—the "Frankish Occupation"—and it would have had a far worse reputation than it does as a period of ethnic and religious subjugation, disenfranchisement, and misery had it not been so quickly followed by the Ottoman conquest and ensuing *Tourkokratia*.

The Turkish conquest has let medievalists too easily off the hook. The *Frangokratia* was in fact a colonial occupation, smaller in scale but no different in kind from the later western colonial conquests of other parts of the world. Efficient foreign armies eliminated the local political leadership, abolished native states, and installed a foreign aristocracy to rule over the locals, who were mostly reduced to a serf-like status and made to serve in foreign economic regimes of exploitation. At best, helpful local elites could rise only to a second-class status within the colonial regimes. Much scholarship focuses on these elites to prove that local support existed for the crusader states. But the latter were ultimately premised on strategies of domination and erected discourses of difference between the conquerors and the natives, including an extreme "othering" of the native, his or her degradation in sexual rhetoric, a highlighting of religious differences, a concern over "mixture" with the natives, and the like. The Latins insisted on calling their subjects Greeks even when the latter insisted on calling themselves Romans. On various levels, the western rulers enforced ethnic and religious distinctions between themselves and the colonized, even though they generally resisted Rome's call for the aggressive conversion of the "Greeks" to Catholicism. Finally, and crucially, they reoriented the local economy to establish, benefit, and entrench western trade routes.

The Crusader occupation was part and parcel of broader processes of western colonialism that were kicking off in this period. This view, however, has not yet been developed. Byzantinists are largely unaware of the potential of post-colonial studies, and Crusades scholarship has, during the past forty years, invested in models that flatter the Crusaders and resist the imputation of any desire for domination to them. Neither group is trained in colonial historiography or post-colonial theory and so they have not discussed this relationship as one of colonial domination. The case has seemed obvious to me for decades, and so I am pleased to see that others too see it this way. A recent book by George Demacopoulos, entitled *Colonizing Christianity: Greek and Latin Religious Identity in the Era of the Fourth Crusade*, takes up this question for the first time.[10] The potential exists here for a library of books and other publications. Assuming that it is forthcoming, will it polarize the two fields even more or finally give them a common ground on which to cooperate? I can imagine both outcomes. (Are we going to continue to white-wash the Crusades?)

This discussion could energize many of the themes raised in this book. Unlike many of the societies colonized by the rising western powers in the early modern period, Byzantium was a far more advanced civilization than the petty baronies of the lords of the Fourth Crusade. It was not only more sophisticated culturally, it was more powerful and wealthy. It had fallen into disarray, which is what the Crusaders exploited, but it was within living memory that Manuel II Komnenos (1143–1180) had played the lords of Europe like pawns and bought them off with his superior wealth. And the glorious sight of Constantinople in 1203 was enough to make these Latins cry in admiration, for all that they wrecked it the following year. Moreover, the culture that they defeated did not merely have a distant and ancient history to be revered, it was, until very recently, the gold standard of Christian king-

---

10 G. E. Demacopoulos, *Colonizing Christianity: Greek and Latin Religious Identity in the Era of the Fourth Crusade* (New York: Fordham University Press, 2019).

ship. It was the direct continuation of the ancient Roman polity and it harboured the legacy of Greek antiquity at levels of scholarship unmatched in the West. The colonizers accordingly erected discourses of ethnic difference, sexual effeminacy, heresy, and decline by which to contain and diminish "the Greeks."

In various forms, these discourses survived until the twentieth century. Byzantium has been systematically excluded from the Roman tradition and from the discipline of classics, even though it was central to the history and identity of both. It has been squeezed out of many rubrics that have been invented to study history, such as late antiquity, the Middle Ages, and (western) Europe and Islam. It is time for it to be unbound from the categories that have been used to contain it.

Further Reading

Suggestions are listed roughly in the order that the topics appear in each chapter. In addition to the texts and studies listed here, see those that are mentioned in the main body and the footnotes of each chapter.

For the Foreword

Beck, Hans-Georg. *Das byzantinische Jahrtausend*. Munich: Beck, 1978.

> The best long introduction to Byzantine civilization, learned and subtle, but unfortunately not yet translated into English.

Treadgold, Warren. *A History of the Byzantine State and Society*. Stanford: Stanford University Press, 1997.

> The most recent, single-authored, long history of Byzantium.

Herrin, Judith. *Byzantium: The Surprising Life of a Medieval Empire*. Princeton: Princeton University Press, 2007.

> The best medium-length introduction to Byzantine civilization in English.

Stathakopoulos, Dionysios. *A Short History of the Byzantine Empire*. London: I. B. Tauris, 2014.

> The most recent short history of Byzantium.

For Chapter 1

Suggested Primary Sources in English Translation

For Roman denialism, see the letter of Louis II to Basileios I, partially trans. by Sheila Ann Ogilvie in Robert Folz, *The Concept of Empire in Western Europe from the Fifth to the Fourteenth Century* (London: Arnold, 1969), 181–84; and fully trans. by Charles West at https://turbulentpriests.group.shef.ac.uk/tag/louis-ii-of-italy/.

For both positive and negative western views in the tenth century, see Liudprand of Cremona, *Antapodosis and Embassy to Constantinople* in *The Complete Works of Liudprand of Cremona*, trans. by Paolo Squatriti (Washington, DC: Catholic University of America Press, 2007).

For western accounts of the Crusades, see *Robert the Monk's History of the First Crusade: Historia Iherosolimitana*, trans. Carol Sweetenham (Farnham: Ashgate, 2005); and Villehardouin, *The Conquest of Constantinople*, in *Joinville and Villehardouin: Chronicles of the Crusades*, trans. by M. R. B. Shaw (London: Penguin, 1963).

The essential Byzantine account of the Fourth Crusade as an atrocity is by Niketas Choniates: Harry J. Magoulias, *O City of Byzantium, Annals of Niketas Choniates* (Detroit: Wayne State University Press, 1984).

For Catholic religious polemic against the eastern Church, see Thomas Aquinas, *Contra Errores Graecorum*, trans. Peter Damian Fehlner and Joseph Kenny at https://dhspriory.org/thomas/ContraErrGraecorum.htm.

For Byzantine "lists of Catholic errors," see the texts translated and discussed in Tia M. Kolbaba, *The Byzantine Lists: Errors of the Latins* (Urbana: University of Illinois Press, 2000).

> There are many, many texts of this kind on both sides, but they tend not to be translated.

The most sophisticated Enlightenment accounts of Byzantium are by Montesquieu, *Considerations on the Causes of the Greatness of the Romans and Their Decline*, trans. David Lowenthal (Indianapolis: Hackett, 1965); and Edward Gibbon, *The History of the Decline and Fall of the Roman Empire*, ed. David Womersley, 3 vols. (London: Penguin, 1994).

> There are plenty of others that are just strings of insults.

Modern Scholarship

Kaldellis, Anthony. *Romanland: Ethnicity and Empire in Byzantium*. Cambridge, MA: Harvard University Press, 2019.

> Shows that the Byzantines were ethnic Romans, and exposes the roots, history, and tactics of western Roman denialism.

Muldoon, James. *Empire and Order: The Concept of Empire, 800–1800*. London: Palgrave 1999.

> A concise survey of western medieval ideas of empire, which, when contrasted to Byzantine ideas, reveals the gulf between the two civilizations.

Ohnsorge, Werner. *Das Zweikaiserproblem im früheren Mittelalter: Die Bedeutung des byzantinischen Reiches für die Entwicklung der Staatsidee in Europa*. Hildesheim: Lax, 1947.

> Classic study of the problem of the "two emperors" (German and Byzantine) and the diplomatic means by which it was never resolved.

Hunger, Herbert. *Graeculus perfidus, Ἰταλὸς ἰταμός: Il senso dell'alterità nei rapporti Greco-Romani ed Italo-Bizantini*. Rome: Unione internazionale degli istituti di archeologia, storia e storia dell'arte in Roma, 1987.

> Brief survey of the stereotypes that Byzantines and western medieval Europeans developed about each other.

Papadakis, Aristeides. *The Christian East and the Rise of the Papacy: The Church 1071–1453 A.D.* Crestwood: St. Vladimir's Seminary Press, 1994.

> Classic study of the relations between the Churches (east and west) during the period when they could no longer pretend to each other that they were unified.

Harris, Jonathan. *Byzantium and the Crusades*, 2nd ed. London: Bloomsbury Academic, 2014.

> Accessible survey of the Byzantine experience of the Crusades, which is usually left out of surveys of the Crusades written by western medievalists.

The Invention of Byzantine Studies in Early Modern Europe, edited by Jake Charles Ransohoff and Nathanael Aschenbrenner (volume in preparation).

> Papers on the emergence of Byzantine Studies in early modern Europe, and a chapter by the present author on the invention of the category "Byzantium" after the Crimean War.

Eisner, Robert. *Travelers to an Antique Land: The History and Literature of Travel to Greece*. Ann Arbor: University of Michigan Press, 1991.

> Accessible introduction to the western travellers to Greece during the Ottoman period.

Yakobaki, Nasia. *Ευρώπη μέσω Ελλάδας: Μια καμπή στην ευρωπαϊκή αυτοσυνείδηση, 17ος–18ος αιώνας*. Athens: Estia, 2006.

> Full analysis of the ideological dimensions of writing about, and travel to, Greece in early European modernity.

Angelov, Dimiter. "Byzantinism: The Imaginary and Real Heritage of Byzantium in Southeastern Europe." In *New Approaches to Balkan Studies*, edited by Dimitris Keridis, Ellen Elias-Bursac, and Nicholas Yatromanolakis, 3–23. Dulles: Brassey's, 2003.

> Insightful study of the ways in which the category "Byzantium" has played out in Balkan ideologies.

Cameron, Averil. "Byzance dans le débat sur orientalisme." In *Byzance en Europe*, edited by Marie-France Auzépy, 235–50. Paris: Presses universitaires de Vincennes, 2003.

> Are Byzantine Studies part of the problem of Orientalism as identified by Edward Said in 1978?

The Reception of Byzantium in European Culture since 1500. Edited by Przemyslaw Marciniak and Dion C. Smythe. Farnham: Ashgate, 2016.

> Wide-ranging collection of papers on theory, art, literature, and history.

For Chapter 2

Suggested Primary Sources in English Translation

For Aileios Aristeides as a proto-Byzantine, read his *Panathenaic Oration*, his oration *To Rome*, and his *Sacred Tales* in *Publius Aelius Aristides: The Complete Works*, trans. Charles Behr, 2 vols. (Leiden: Brill, 1981–1986).

For the articulation of these elements in an early Byzantine form, see Synesios of Kyrene's *On Kingship* (on Roman governance), *Dion Or on My Way of Life* (on Hellenism), and *Letter* 105 (his terms for agreeing to become a bishop) in *The Letters of Synesius of Cyrene*, trans. Augustine FitzGerald (London: Oxford University Press 1926); and *The Essays and Hymns of Synesius of Cyrene, including the Address to the Emperor Arcadius and the Political Speeches*, trans. Augustine FitzGerald, 2 vols. (London: Oxford University Press 1930).

For Byzantine history as Roman history, read the twelfth-century verse chronicle by Konstantinos Manasses (the *Historical Synopsis*) in *The Chronicle of Constantine Manasses*, trans. Linda Yuretich (Liverpool: Liverpool University Press, 2018).

For the continuity of Greek literature in Byzantine eyes, see the book reviews and literary essays by Photios, *Ten Thousand Books* (ninth century), partially translated in *Photius: The Bibliotheca*, trans. Nigel Wilson (London: Duckworth, 1994), and Theodoros Metochites, *The Essays* (fourteenth century), in *Theodore Metochites on Ancient Authors and Philosophy: Semeioseis gnomikai 1-26 & 71*, trans. Karin Hult (Göteborg: Acta Universitatis Gothoburgensis, 2002).

For a chronicle that situates Byzantium between the Latin West and the Islamic world, with partial coverage of both in the seventh and eighth centuries, see Theophanes, *Chronographia, The Chronicle of Theophanes Confessor, Byzantine and Near Eastern History AD 284-813*, trans. Cyril Mango and Roger Scott (Oxford: Oxford University Press, 1997).

Modern Scholarship

Obolensky, Dimitri. *The Byzantine Commonwealth, Eastern Europe, 500-1453*. London: Weidenfeld and Nicolson 1971.
> Magisterial survey of the early influence of Byzantium in the formation of Slavic Orthodox cultures, albeit largely oblivious to its Roman character.

Brague, Rémi. *Eccentric Culture: A Theory of Western Civilization*. South Bend: St Augustine's Press, 2002.
> On defining western (or Catholic?) Europe as a Roman (but non-Byzantine) space.

Kaldellis, Anthony. *Hellenism in Byzantium: The Transformations of Greek Identity and the Reception of the Classical Tradition*. Cambridge: Cambridge University Press, 2007.

> Considers Byzantium as an articulation of Greek, Roman, and Christian elements in various combinations, especially the Romanization of the Greeks.

——. *The Christian Parthenon: Pilgrimage and Classicism in Byzantine Athens*. Cambridge: Cambridge University Press, 2009.

> The Parthenon as both classical-Hellenic and Byzantine-Orthodox.

Siniossoglou, Niketas. *Radical Platonism in Byzantium: Illumination and Utopia in Gemistos Plethon*. Cambridge: Cambridge University Press, 2011.

> The enduring vitality of Hellenic pagan thought in later Byzantium.

Dagron, Gilbert. "Aux origines de la civilization byzantine: Langue de culture et langue d'État." *Revue historique* 241 (1969): 23–56.

> Preliminary study of how Greek, Latin, and Latin-inflected Greek found their respective spaces in the articulation of Byzantine society.

Harris, William V. *Roman Power: A Thousand Years of Empire*. Cambridge: Cambridge University Press, 2016.

> Broad sweep of Roman history that explicitly includes Byzantium, and raises the question of whether it was constituted as a "Roman nation."

Neville, Leonora. *Guide to Byzantine Historical Writing*. Cambridge: Cambridge University Press, 2018.

> An excellent survey of how Byzantine historiography directly continued ancient Greek and Roman traditions.

Horrocks, Geoffrey. *Greek: A History of the Language and its Speakers*. Chichester: Wiley, 2014.

> The linguistic history of Byzantine Greek within the overall evolution of the Greek language from antiquity to today.

The Oxford Handbook of the Second Sophistic. Edited by Daniel S. Richter and William A. Johnson. Oxford: Oxford University Press, 2017.

> The Greek literature of the Second Sophistic period formed the immediate matrix for the emergence of Byzantine literature, both Christian and pagan.

The Oxford Handbook of Late Antiquity. Edited by Scott Fitzgerald Johnson. Oxford: Oxford University Press, 2016.

> Scholarly reference-book for the field of late antique studies, which ranges from the second to the eighth centuries and from the medieval west to Central Asia.

Giardina, Andrea. "Esplosione di tardoantico." *Studi storici* 40, no. 1 (1999): 157–80.

> There have been many critiques of the category of "late antiquity," but this was the first serious one, questioning the field's ever-expanding horizons and blindness to institutional history.

For Chapter 3

Suggested Primary Sources in English Translation

For Byzantine readings of ancient literature, including historiography, see the texts by Photios and Metochites cited in the suggestions for Chapter 2, above; also the texts in Anthony Kaldellis, *Byzantine Readings of Ancient Historians: Texts in Translation, with Introductions and Notes* (London: Routledge, 2015); and Charles Barber and Stratis Papaioannou, *Michael Psellos on Literature and Art: A Byzantine Perspective on Aesthetics* (Notre Dame: University of Notre Dame Press, 2017).

For Christian attempts to grapple with the problems of pagan literature, see Basileios of Kaisareia (Basil of Caesarea), *To Young Men on How They Might Benefit from Greek Literature* in *Saint Basil: The Letters*, ed. and trans. R. J. Deferrari and M. R. P. McGuire, 4 vols. (Cambridge, MA: Loeb Classical Library, 1934), 4:363–435; *Saint Basil on the Value of Greek Literature*, ed. and commentary by Nigel G. Wilson (London: Duckworth, 1975); also *A Christian's Guide to Greek Culture: The Pseudo-Nonnus Commentaries on Sermons 4, 5, 39 and 43 by Gregory of Nazianzus*, trans. Jennifer Nimmo Smith (Liverpool: Liverpool University Press, 2001).

Byzantine classical scholarship is usually too technical to be translated for general audiences. The *Souda* is now translated online: www.stoa.org/sol/. For commentaries and interpretations (the latter usually allegorical), see Eustathios of Thessalonike, *Commentary on Homer's Odyssey*, ed. Eric Cullhed (Uppsala: Uppsala Universitet, 2016); and John Tzetzes, *Allegories of the Iliad*, trans. Adam J.

Goldwyn and Dimitra Kokkini, Dumbarton Oaks Medieval Library 37 (Cambridge, MA: Harvard University Press, 2015).

Modern Scholarship

Reynolds, L. D., and N. G. Wilson, *Scribes and Scholars: A Guide to the Transmission of Greek and Latin Literature*, 4th ed. Oxford: Oxford University Press, 2014.

> Outstanding survey of the transmission of ancient literature that covers both the Latin west and the Greek east.

Cavallo, Guglielmo. *Lire à Byzance*, trans. by Paolo Odorico and Alain Segonds. Paris: Belles Lettres, 2006.

> The culture of reading in Byzantium, both secular and religious, including how it was shaped by the Byzantine book.

Hunger, Herbert. *Schreiben und Lesen in Byzanz: Die byzantinische Buchkultur*. Munich: Beck, 1989.

> Still the best synthesis of Byzantine book culture.

Kaldellis, Anthony. "The Byzantine Role in the Making of the Corpus of Classical Greek Historiography: A Preliminary Investigation." *Journal of Hellenic Studies* 132 (2012): 71–85.

> An example of how Byzantine tastes and intellectual needs shaped the survival of the classical canon (focusing on historiography).

Ronconi, Filippo, *La traslitterazione dei testi greci: Una ricerca tra paleografia e filologia*. Spoleto: Fondazione Centro italiano di studi sull'alto Medioevo, 2003.

> Technical study of how Greek texts were copied into the new minuscule script after ca. 800, a bottleneck in their transmission.

Dickey, Eleanor. *Ancient Greek Scholarship: A Guide to Finding, Reading, and Understanding Scholia, Commentaries, Lexica, and Grammatical Treatises, from Their Beginnings to the Byzantine Period*. American Philological Association classical resources series 7. Oxford: Oxford University Press, 2007.

> Indispensible study, the title says it all.

Kaldellis, Anthony. "Classical Scholarship in Twelfth-Century Byzantium." In *Medieval Greek Commentaries on the* Nicomachean Ethics, edited by Charles Barber and David Jenkins, 1–43. Leiden: Brill, 2009.

> Survey of the modes of Byzantine classical scholarship in one of its most productive periods.

Bourbouhakis, Manolis. "Byzantine Literary Criticism and the Classical Heritage." In *The Cambridge Intellectual History of Byzantium*, edited by Anthony Kaldellis and Niketas Siniossoglou, 113–28. Cambridge: Cambridge University Press, 2017.

> The various ways in which Byzantine writers and scholars engaged with ancient texts.

Bassett, Sarah. *The Urban Image of Late Antique Constantinople*. Cambridge: Cambridge University Press, 2004.

> The placement, ideological use, and various interpretations of classical art in early Constantinople (mostly fourth century AD).

Momigliano, Arnaldo. *Studies on Modern Scholarship*, edited by Glen W. Bowersock and T. J. Cornell. Berkeley: University of California Press, 1994.

> Portraits of great classicists of the nineteenth century, showing (incidentally, not on purpose) that they regularly handled and even published on Byzantine materials.

For Chapter 4

Suggested Primary Sources in English Translation

For early positive Byzantine views of the Franks, see Agathias (sixth century) in *Agathias: The Histories*, trans. Joseph D. Frendo (Berlin: de Gruyter, 1975), especially bk. 1; and Konstantinos VII Porphyrogennetos (tenth century) in *Constantine Porphyrogenitus: De administrando imperio*, ed. Gyula Moravcsik and trans. Romilly Jenkins (Washington, DC: Dumbarton Oaks, 1967), especially Chapter 13.

For negative later Byzantine views of the Franks, see Anna Komnene, *Alexiad* (twelfth century), trans. E. R. A. Sweter and rev. by P. Frankopan (London: Penguin, 2009), especially the account of the First Crusade in books 10–12; and Niketas Choniates (early thirteenth century) in *O City of Byzantium, Annals of Niketas Choniates*, trans. Harry J. Magoulias (Detroit: Wayne State University Press, 1984), especially the account of the Third and Fourth Crusades in the last third of the work.

Few Byzantine anti-Catholic theological treatises have been translated: see Photios, *On the Mystagogy of the Holy Spirit by Saint Photius, Patriarch of Constantinople* (Astoria: Holy Transfiguration Monastery, 1983) (ninth century); and the texts in T. Kolbaba, "Meletios Homologetes, *On The Customs of the Italians*," *Revue des études byzantines* 55 (1997): 137–68 (thirteenth century); and "Barlaam the Calabrian, *Three Treatises on Papal Primacy*," *Revue des études byzantines* 53 (1995): 41–115 (fourteenth century). A fourteenth-century Byzantine who converted to Catholicism, Demetrios Kydones, wrote a work to encourage his country-men to be accept the Latins. This rare pro-Catholic treatise exposes the grounds for Byzantine anti-Latin suspicion: trans. in J. Likoudis, *Ending the Byzantine Greek Schism, Containing: The 14th Century Apologia of Demetrios Kydones for Unity with Rome and the "Contra Errores Graecorum" of St. Thomas Aquinas*, 2nd ed. (New Rochelle: Catholics United for the Faith, 1992).

The Latin colonial presence in Greece is celebrated in the *Chronicle of the Morea* in *Crusaders as Conquerors: the Chronicle of Morea*, trans. H. E. Lurier (New York: Columbia University Press, 1964).

Modern Scholarship

Baum, Wilhelm, and Dietmar W. Winkler, *The Church of the East: A Concise History*. London: Routledge, 2003.

> A useful corrective for medievalists who think that the West formed a large part of the Christian world in the early Middle Ages.

Wickham, Chris, *The Inheritance of Rome: Illuminating the Dark Age, 400–1000*. London: Viking, 2009.

> Accessible narrative that treats the medieval West, Byzantium, and the Islamic world in parallel as heirs of the old Roman empire.

Kaldellis, Anthony. *Ethnography after Antiquity: Foreign Lands and People in Byzantine Literature*. Philadelphia: University of Pennsylvania Press, 2013.

> Late Byzantine views of the "Franks" or "Latins" are treated in detail on pp. 166–83.

Whittow, Mark. "The Second Fall: The Place of the Eleventh Century in Roman History." In *Byzantium in the Eleventh Century: Being in Between*, edited by Marc D. Lauxterman and Mark Whittow. London: Routledge, 2017.

Lucid and accessible argument setting forth the institutional reasons why eleventh-century Byzantium *was* the Roman empire, unlike almost every polity in the medieval West. See esp. pp. 112–14.

Smith, Julia M. H. *Europe after Rome: A New Cultural History 500–1000*. Oxford: Oxford University Press, 2005.

Wide-ranging survey of the many ways in which western medieval people engaged with the Roman tradition and used it as a medium to articulate a common culture (that excluded Byzantium, we must add).

Patlagean, Évelyne. *Un Moyen Âge grec: Byzance IXe–XVe siècle*. Paris: Albin Michel, 2007.

An attempt to fold Byzantium into a western medieval paradigm through the concept of feudalism.

Runciman, Steven. *A History of the Crusades*. 3 vols. Cambridge: Cambridge University Press, 1951.

What the Crusades looked like from the perspective of a historian who knew the Christian East, before their partisan rehabilitation among western scholars that set in a few decades ago.

Lock, Peter. *The Franks in the Aegean*. London: Longman, 1995.

Solid survey of what Greeks call the "Frangokratia" (period of Frankish rule) written by a western medieval scholar from a western point of view and using mostly western sources; does not see this as a phase of western colonialism.

Demacopoulos, George. *Colonizing Christianity: Greek and Latin Religious Identity in the Era of the Fourth Crusade*. New York: Fordham University Press 2019.

Explicit study of the Frangokratia as a western colonial project and its impact on the Byzantines as such.

Printed and bound by CPI Group (UK) Ltd, Croydon, CR0 4YY

25/03/2025

14647339-0004